Oxford School *Shakespeare*

THE TAMING
of the SHREW

edited by
Roma Gill, OBE
M.A. *Cantab.*, B. Litt. *Oxon*

OXFORD
UNIVERSITY PRESS

OXFORD

UNIVERSITY PRESS

Great Clarendon Street, Oxford OX2 6DP

Oxford University Press is a department of the University of Oxford.
It furthers the University's objective of excellence in research, scholarship, and
education by publishing worldwide in

Oxford New York

Auckland Bangkok Buenos Aires Cape Town Chennai Dar es Salaam Delhi
Hong Kong Istanbul Karachi Kolkata Kuala Lumpur Madrid Melbourne
Mexico City Mumbai Nairobi São Paulo Shanghai Taipei Tokyo Toronto

Oxford is a registered trade mark of Oxford University Press
in the UK and in certain other countries

Illustrations by Alexy Pendle

Cover photograph by Robbie Jack shows Josie Lawrence as Katherina and
Michael Siberry as Petruchio in the Royal Shakespeare Company's 1995
production of *The Taming of the Shrew*. All inside photographs (except p. 133) by
Donald Cooper/Photostage.

For Laura

Oxford School Shakespeare
edited by Roma Gill

Typeset by Herb Bowes Graphics, Oxford
Printed and bound by Creative Print and Design Wales, Ebbw Vale

Contents

Introduction

About the Play

On stage and on screen *The Taming of the Shrew* is an outstanding comic success. In performance, the characters are instantly recognizable; and all the disguisings and mistakings, which seem so laborious when they are explained to a reader, are immediately apparent to an *audience*. When the play is acted, it moves with great speed through the complications of its plot. Spectators are probably not conscious of the extreme complexity of the plotting and characterization—a complexity which is even more remarkable when we remember that this is one of Shakespeare's earliest plays, and perhaps his first attempt at writing a comedy!

The Taming of the Shrew could be described as 'an-action-within-a-plot-within-a-deception'. The 'deception' involves a tinker—Christopher Sly—and an English nobleman. The 'plot' concerns an Italian gentleman—Lucentio—and his efforts to win the fair Bianca to be his wife. And the 'action' is Petruchio's 'taming' of the 'shrew', Katherina.

Leading Characters in the Play

1 THE DECEPTION

Christopher Sly   a drunken peasant in Warwickshire (England) who is persuaded that he is a nobleman.

Lord   a real nobleman, who plays a trick on Sly.

2 THE PLOT

Lucentio   a young gentleman visiting Padua, who falls in love with Bianca.

Baptista   a wealthy citizen of Padua who wants to find suitable husbands for his two daughters.

Katherina   Baptista's elder daughter, who seems unlikely to get a husband because of her bad temper (but see 'The Action', below).

Bianca   Baptista's younger daughter; Hortensio and Gremio both want to marry her, and Lucentio falls in love with her.

Petruchio   Hortensio's friend, visiting Padua in search of a rich wife (see 'The Action', below).

3 THE ACTION

Katherina   Baptista's elder daughter, whose intelligence and independence make her resent the way she is treated by her father and her sister's suitors. She challenges Petruchio, but is finally persuaded to accept his superior strength.

Petruchio   a stranger from Verona, who has come to Padua hoping to find a rich wife. He engages in a battle with Katherina, refusing to let her rest until she gives in to him.

Synopsis

INDUCTION

Scene 1 Christopher Sly, in a drunken sleep outside an English country pub, is discovered by a noble Lord returning from a day's hunting. The Lord decides to play a trick on Sly. He takes him home, and instructs the servants to treat Sly as though he were a nobleman who has been sick and out of his mind. A company of travelling players arrives at the Lord's house.

Scene 2 Sly wakes up, and is persuaded to watch the actors perform their play—which is:

The Taming of the Shrew.

ACT 1

Scene 1 Lucentio arrives in Padua with his manservant, Tranio. They encounter Baptista with his two daughters, Katherina and Bianca. Baptista insists that a husband must be found for Katherina (the elder daughter) before he will allow anyone to marry Bianca. Bianca's suitors, Hortensio and Gremio, call a truce in their rivalry for Bianca's love—but now Lucentio has fallen in love with her, too. He decides to change places with Tranio, so that he can attend on Bianca disguised as a schoolmaster—whilst Tranio (calling himself 'Lucentio') will also present himself as a suitor to Bianca.

Scene 2 Petruchio arrives in Padua with his servant, Grumio. They call on Hortensio, and Petruchio explains that he is hoping to find a rich wife. When he hears about Katherina, Petruchio declares that she will be the right wife for him!

Whilst they are talking, Gremio comes along with Lucentio, who is now disguised as a schoolmaster (calling himself 'Cambio'). Gremio and Hortensio renew their rivalry for Bianca's love—and they are joined by a third competitor, who calls himself 'Lucentio' (but who, in fact, is Tranio in disguise).

ACT 2

Scene 1   Katherina and Bianca are quarrelling. Tranio ('Lucentio') and Petruchio introduce themselves to Baptista, and Petruchio begins his wooing of Katherina. They fight, but he is determined to marry her. Gremio and Tranio ('Lucentio') make bids for the hand of Bianca; Gremio is defeated—but 'Lucentio' must get his father to secure the promises he has made.

ACT 3

Scene 1   Bianca's suitors present themselves to her as tutors: Lucentio is disguised as 'Cambio', and Hortensio is the musician, 'Litio'.

Scene 2   On the wedding day, Baptista waits with his daughters (and Bianca's suitors) for the arrival of Katherina's bridegroom. Biondello describes Petruchio's appearance, and the bridal party goes off to the church. Lucentio and Tranio stay behind. Gremio returns to report what has happened in the church. Petruchio and Katherina—now married—come back with their friends; but Petruchio refuses to wait for the marriage-feast, and he insists on carrying away his bride.

ACT 4

Scene 1   Petruchio's servants are preparing to receive their master and his new wife. Grumio describes their journey from Padua. Petruchio complains about their dinner, and Katherina goes hungry to bed. Petruchio outlines the method he will use for 'taming' his 'shrew'.

Scene 2   Hortensio ('Litio') and Tranio ('Lucentio') listen whilst the *real* Lucentio ('Cambio') courts Bianca. They both agree to withdraw from the competition for Bianca's love, and Hortensio announces that he is going to marry a rich widow. Tranio tells Lucentio that he has won Bianca—provided that he can get his father's support (which Baptista demanded in *Act* 2, *Scene* 1). A passing Merchant is persuaded to impersonate Vincentio, Lucentio's father.

Scene 3   Petruchio continues the 'taming' of Katherina, refusing to let her eat, and sending away her new clothes. He plans to return to Baptista's house—but will not go until Katherina agrees with him in everything he says.

Scene 4   Tranio ('Lucentio') introduces the Merchant—who is pretending to be his father ('Vincentio')—to Baptista. They go to draw up the marriage-settlement for Bianca. Biondello tells the *real* Lucentio ('Cambio') that he must now take Bianca to the church and find a priest to marry them.

Scene 5   Katherina tries once more to contradict her husband, then finally concedes victory to Petruchio. They depart for Padua, and on the way they meet the *real* Vincentio, the father of Lucentio.

ACT 5

Scene 1   Lucentio and Bianca hurry off to the church. Petruchio, Katherina, and the *real* Vincentio arrive at Lucentio's house, but the Merchant (who is *pretending* to be Lucentio's father) refuses to let them in. Lucentio and Bianca, newly married, return; and the false identities are revealed.

Scene 2   A marriage-feast has been enjoyed, honouring three wedded couples: Petruchio and Katherina; Lucentio and Bianca; Hortensio and his wealthy Widow. The three brides leave the room, and the husbands lay bets on which of their wives will prove the most obedient. Katherina wins the wager for Petruchio, and delivers a lecture on the proper duty of a wife to her husband.

The Taming of the Shrew: commentary

1. THE DECEPTION

Shakespeare is on home ground at the opening of his play, setting the scene in Warwickshire, not far from where he was born in Stratford-upon-Avon. The geography is clear from the tinker Sly's reference to his origin at 'Burton-heath' and his acquaintance with 'Marian Hacket the fat ale-wife of Wincot'—who was quite possibly a real person. Both Sly and the unnamed Lord returning from the day's hunting are, we can assume, fairly typical of their contemporaries in Elizabethan society. The distinction of social classes is marked as soon as the Lord speaks, and the Huntsmen reply to him, in the blank verse used dramatically to indicate superior characters or elevated topics.[1] The contrast between the 'prosaic' Sly and the 'poetic' Lord is further emphasized when the Huntsmen are given directions for Sly's accommodation in 'the fairest chamber', and the play-acting theme is heightened by the arrival of the actors' touring company.

Such strolling players were regular visitors to English country houses (and country inns) during the summer months. The London theatres were usually closed to avoid the spreading of infectious diseases, and the actors must tour, or else disband their companies. The Lord is familiar with the company—and also it seems, with some contemporary acting techniques. He directs his page to play the Lady's part, just as any boy-actor would perform female roles in the Elizabethan theatre (where apprentice boys always acted the women's parts), and we also learn the correct behaviour for a lady, who should present herself 'With soft low tongue and lowly courtesy'.

Two cultures collide when Sly wakes and tries to establish his own identity and social sphere against the opposition of the Servingmen who try to convince him of his noble origins. The Servingmen are successful—partly, perhaps, because Sly has always aspired to the nobility: after all, he told the Hostess who threw him out of her ale-house that his family 'came in with Richard Conqueror'. When Sly has accepted his new role (even attempting to speak in the appropriate manner), Shakespeare manipulates the characters—just for a laugh— into a tricky situation in which the tinker insists that his new-found 'lady' should come to bed. The arrival of the players rescues the terrified

[1] See 'Shakespeare's Verse', p. xvi.

Bartholomew, and sustains the Lord's deception with their own illusion—*their* play. Sly—who has taken the leading part until now—retires to become, together with the Lord and the Servingmen, an audience for a completely new play. He is allowed some critical comment on the scene that follows—'"Tis a very excellent piece of work, madam lady. Would 'twere done!'—and then Sly, with the Lord's deception, is forgotten.[2]

2.   THE PLOT

All that we have already learned about the Warwickshire Lord and the manner of his living—the courtly behaviour of his servants and the refined elegance of his furnishings and pictures—should lead us to expect that he will have an equally sophisticated taste in drama. Fortunately, the players are able to provide suitable entertainment. Their play, which tells the story of Lucentio, is loosely based on a classical Italian comedy, *I Suppositi* (The Imposters) by Ariosto, which was translated into English by George Gascoigne in 1566 and given the title *Supposes*. The *dramatis personae* of *Supposes* are the stock characters of the Latin comedy, and so is the theme—the attempt of a young man (aided by his clever servant) to secure the girl he loves, although her father favours a rival who is richer—and much older.

The first exchanges between Lucentio and Tranio make sure that we know that the scene is now Italy—Padua—and that these are 'really' actors. They speak formal blank verse, in contrast to the relaxed idiom of Sly's speeches, and speak for the audience to hear, not to converse with each other. The atmosphere relaxes, becoming more 'natural', when Baptista, his daughters, and Bianca's suitors erupt on to the scene, producing a little drama for which Lucentio and Tranio become the audience, until finally Lucentio decides to join the rival suitors and be a competitor for Bianca's love—whilst Tranio, disguised as his master, plays the part of Lucentio. In later scenes Tranio tries to speak as though he were indeed the master and not a servant: his use of learned similes and contorted syntax should be taken as the equivalent of an upper-class accent:

> Fair Leda's daughter had a thousand wooers;
> Then well one more may fair Bianca have.
> And so she shall: Lucentio shall make one,
> Though Paris came in hope to speed alone.   *1, 2, 238–41*

Tranio is 'talking posh'.

[2] See Appendix A, p. 114.

The confrontation of the rival suitors comes in *Act 2*, Scene 1, when Gremio and the supposed Lucentio (who is Tranio in disguise), compete for Bianca's hand in response to her father's promise that 'he of both That can assure my daughter greatest dower Shall have my Bianca's love'. It seems that Bianca is being sold to the highest bidder—but this is not, in fact, the case.

It was the duty of an Elizabethan father to look after his daughter, making certain that she married a husband who would be able to support her in comfort and who would be generous in providing for his wife's future should he himself die. The Elizabethan lady had few legal rights: when she married, she and everything she owned (the money she inherited from her father, for instance) became the property of her husband—and there were no careers open to women.

Baptista is acting responsibly—although, of course, he is being duped by Tranio. His conduct here, in arranging the marriage of Bianca (their father's 'treasure', according to Katherina in 2, 1, 32) justifies his earlier treatment of his elder daughter, when he accepted Petruchio's offer of marriage in what seems to be the main business of *The Taming of the Shrew*.

3. THE ACTION—THE TAMING OF THE SHREW

Stories of nagging and unruly wives—shrews—are common in folk tales and early ballad literature, but Shakespeare seems to have no particular source for his story of Katherina and Petruchio. In popular fiction the husband's triumph is secured (to male applause) through the use of brute force—but Shakespeare is sparing with physical violence. Early in their courtship Katherina tempts her suitor by striking him when he claims to be a gentleman—but Petruchio contents himself with warning 'I swear I'll cuff you if you strike again' (2, 1, 217). And his warning is heeded.

In many respects, however, Petruchio's method of 'taming' Katherina resembles those of his traditional predecessors. He insists on a period of disorientation and disruption, dragging his bride away from her home and her wedding-feast to endure a perilous journey to his remote country house. Arriving there, cold and tired, she is refused food and denied rest—and all the time Petruchio assures her that he is acting in her best interests. When at last she leaves the stage, Petruchio takes the audience into his confidence and explains his technique in terms that would be familiar enough to the sporting Elizabethans: Katherina is his 'falcon', and it is necessary for him to 'man [his] haggard'—the wild bird must be made gentle, subdued to the will of the trainer yet still keen to hunt and catch the prey. A novel of the late twentieth century[3] describes the process most effectively—though here the would-be falconer is a small boy, training and treasuring a young kestrel that had fallen from its nest (see Appendix B, p.117).

In the management of Katherina there are three stages, and each one is signalled by a kiss. The first kiss is that of a triumphant hunter who has secured his bird. On his very first appearance Petruchio openly stated his intention 'to wive it wealthily in Padua', and not all his friend's warnings can shake his resolution. He is not even deterred by the exhibition of Katherina's temper when she breaks the lute over Hortensio's head. When Katherina comes to meet him on the stage, Petruchio advances warily, as though stalking his prey; then he gently caresses her with words of love. Katherina struggles, at first verbally and then with attempted physical strength—which Petruchio easily resists. Another round of insults is followed by more loving words, and after a brief final round Petruchio assumes the victor's part: 'I must and will have Katherina for my wife'. Petruchio sustains the new role he has created for himself until the formalities with Baptista are concluded, and he can celebrate the first part of his conquest: 'kiss me, Kate, we will be married o' Sunday'.

This kiss is almost a violation. Katherina does not speak; she leaves the stage at the same time as Petruchio, but probably at a different stage door.

The second kiss is a different matter. It is first asked, then refused, and then allowed. Katherina has endured the shame of her marriage to a disorderly ruffian, and suffered the deprivations of her new home life. She has even allowed Petruchio to determine sun and moon—the day and the night—for her:

> . . . sun it is not, when you say it is not,
> And the moon changes even as your mind

—although the second line here permits her to impute a degree of lunacy to her husband's conduct. Her obedience has been tested in the embarrassing encounter with the fellow-traveller (who proves to be Vincentio, the father of Lucentio), and she has shown a new charm—even a sense of fun—in sharing in her husband's deception. For Petruchio, this was a kind of 'trial run', to test the success of his training.

The relationship between Katherina and Petruchio has changed. We know this when the party arrives outside Lucentio's house, where the real Vincentio confronts the supposed Vincentio. As soon as the

[3] *A Kestrel for a Knave*, 1968, by Barry Hines; the book was later made into a film, *Kes*.

comedy begins, Petruchio draws his wife to the side: 'Prithee, Kate, let's stand aside and see the end of this controversy'. In becoming an audience, apart from the action they are now watching, Katherina and Petruchio are brought together: their separation from the other characters emphasizes their mutual togetherness.

And the second kiss, which comes at the end of *Act 5*, Scene 1, when there is only a servant to witness it, is the kiss of confederates. Petruchio and Katherina are ready for their big scene.

The joyous celebration of a triple wedding needs no explanation. A note of discord is struck by Hortensio's widow, a character who seems to have been something of an afterthought on Shakespeare's part. The spirited exchange between her and Katherina shows Petruchio's 'taming' has not broken his wife's spirit—but now both husband and wife enjoy the wrangling that ensues. It is a game, one that all the husbands relish—especially when it develops into the testing situation where the men can lay their bets, each backing his own wife against the other two women. What starts as homely festival fun becomes serious when Katherina wins Petruchio's bet for him. For the theatre audience, the outcome of the wager was never in doubt; the defeated husbands take their losses in good part, and the wives enjoy their discomfiture— when Lucentio rues his loss, Bianca has no sympathy: 'The more fool you for laying on my duty'. But then Petruchio takes charge, and puts Katherina in the position of command to deliver his lecture, the fruits of her learned experience.

The speech is made up of Elizabethan commonplaces about the duty of a wife—utterances which have their basis in the marriage service of the Church of England and in the homily 'Of the State of Matrimony' which was preached annually;[4] ultimately, of course, these derive from the authority of the New Testament. Modern audience reactions to this speech are many and varied—as indeed are the emphases of actresses and theatrical directors. The lines have been delivered with heavy irony, implying that Petruchio's triumph is illusory; or with spiritless submission, suggesting that the victory has been dearly bought, and that 'a Kate Conformable as other household Kates' (2, 1, 269–70) is really not much fun.

I myself prefer to take the speech at its face value, recognizing its historical context and its general truths, and anticipating the third kiss, which announces the consummation of a relationship: 'Come on and kiss me, Kate . . .

4 See 'Background', p. 130.

Come, Kate, we'll to bed.
We three are married, but you two are sped.'

The play limps disappointingly in its final couplet, tempting a critic to refer to Shakespeare's inexperience as a dramatist at the time he wrote *The Taming of the Shrew* (>1592), and suggesting that he was not in perfect control of the very complicated material that he had chosen to work with. We have come a long way from the Warwickshire (England) alehouse of the Induction's first scene; Christopher Sly, the trickster Lord, and the touring actors have all been forgotten in the interest generated by the play's 'real' characters—a man, and a boy dressed as a woman, whose action and moral dilemmas are more important today than they were to their first audience.

Shakespeare's Verse

Easily the best way to understand and appreciate Shakespeare's verse is to read it aloud—and don't worry if you don't understand everything! Try not to be captivated by the dominant rhythm, but decide which are the most important words in each line and use the regular metre to drive them forward to the listeners.

Shakespeare's plays are mainly written in 'blank verse', the form preferred by most dramatists in the sixteenth and early seventeenth centuries. It is a very flexible medium, which is capable—like the human speaking voice—of a wide range of tones. Basically the lines, which are unrhymed, are ten syllables long. The syllables have alternating stresses, just like normal English speech; and they divide into five 'feet'. The technical name for this is 'iambic pentameter'.

> **Lord**
> What's hére? One déad, or drúnk? See, dóth he bréathe?
> **Second Huntsman**
> He bréathes, my lórd. Were hé not wárm'd with ále,
> This wére a béd but cóld to sléep so sóundly.
> **Lord**
> O mónstrous béast, how líke a swíne he líes!
> Grim déath, how fóul and loáthsome ís thine ímage!
> Sirs, Í will práctise ón this drúnken mán.
> What thínk you, íf he wére convéy'd to béd.
> Wrapp'd ín sweet clóthes, rings pút upón his fíngers,
> A móst delícious bánquet bý his béd,
> And bráve atténdants néar him whén he wákes—
> Would nót the béggar thén forgét himsélf?
> **First Huntsman**
> Belíeve me, lórd, I thínk he cánnot chóose.

> (Induction, 1, 27–38)

The pentameter accommodates a variety of speech tones—the Lord's surprise when he discovers Sly in his drunken sleep, his disgust when he realizes what he has found, and his delight in the practical joke that he plans. The Huntsman replies politely to his master; and the regularity of his lines shows him to belong to the Lord's society. Although he is a servant, he is not—like Sly and the Hostess—a peasant.

In this quotation, the lines are mainly regular in length and normal in iambic stress pattern. Sometimes Shakespeare deviates from the norm, writing lines that are longer or shorter than ten syllables, and varying the stress patterns for unusual emphasis—as in the Lord's cry of exaggerated horror, 'Grim déath, how fóul and loáthsome ís thine ímage!'. The verse line sometimes contains the grammatical unit of meaning—'O mónstrous béast, how líke a swíne he líes!'—thus allowing for a pause at the end of the line, before a new idea is started; at other times, the sense runs on from one line to the next, as it does in lines 120–1, where the Lord speaks of 'a wóman's gíft To ráin a shówer óf commánded téars'. This makes for the natural fluidity of speech, avoiding monotony but still maintaining the iambic rhythm.

Source, Date, and Text

Shakespeare took his raw material for *The Taming of the Shrew* from a variety of sources. The deception of Christopher Sly derives ultimately from *The Arabian Nights*. Shakespeare could have read a version of this in a collection of stories by Richard Edwards, which was published in 1570 but which is now lost. Lucentio's plot to win Bianca comes from George Gascoigne's *Supposes* (1566), which is itself a translation of *I Suppositi* by Ariosto. No single source has been found for the main action, although it is possible that Shakespeare knew the ballad of *A Shrewde and Curste Wyfe* which was published in 1550. Here, as in Shakespeare's play, the 'shrew' is compared to a docile sister, her wedding is disrupted, and she is similarly deprived of food.

It is impossible to assign a precise date to *The Taming of the Shrew*. Shakespeare's play is clearly related to an anonymous play, *The Taming of A Shrew*, and it seems most likely that the unknown author was the borrower, and that *A Shrew* is later than *The Shrew*. *A Shrew* was published in 1594 and may have been written as early as 1592. *The Taming of the Shrew* was not published until 1623, when it appeared in the collection of Shakespeare's plays which is known as the First Folio. The present edition uses the text established by Ann Thompson for the New Cambridge Shakespeare (1984).

Characters in the Play

The Induction in WARWICKSHIRE

Christopher Sly	*a tinker*
Hostess	*at the alehouse*
Lord	
Bartholomew	*the* Lord's *page*
Huntsmen	
and	*attending the* Lord
Servingmen	
Actors	*visiting the* Lord, *and playing the parts of the characters in*

THE TAMING OF THE SHREW

THE FATHERS	
Baptista Minola	*a rich citizen of Padua*
Vincentio	*a merchant from Pisa*
THE DAUGHTERS	
Katherina	*the 'shrew', Baptista's elder daughter*
Bianca	Baptista's *younger daughter*
THE SUITORS	
Gremio	*a rich old man of Padua*
Hortensio	*a gentleman of Padua*
Lucentio	*a gentleman from Pisa*
Petruchio	*a gentleman from Verona*
THE SERVANTS	
Tranio	*servant to* Lucentio
Biondello	Lucentio's *boy*
Grumio	*servant to* Petruchio
Curtis	*servant at* Petruchio's *house*
ALSO	**Tailor, Haberdasher, Merchant from Mantua, Widow, Additional Servants**

The scene of the play is Italy

INDUCTION

Induction Scene 1
Christopher Sly is thrown out of the tavern, and discovered by a passing nobleman who decides to play a trick on him with the help of a company of travelling players.

Induction Shakespeare's only use of a popular opening device is soon forgotten: see 'Source, Date, and Text', p.xviii.

1 *feeze you*: fix you, sort you out.
2 *pair of stocks*: The Hostess threatens to punish Sly by having him confined in the stocks.

4 *Chronicles*: history books.
we . . . Conqueror: In his attempt to impress the Hostess with his aristocratic origins (but making an obvious error with 'Richard' for 'William the Conqueror'), Sly unwittingly anticipates the trick that will be played on him.
5 *paucas pallabris*: few words; Sly uses a catchphrase (Spanish *pocas palabras*) from one of the most famous plays of the time, *The Spanish Tragedy*, by Thomas Kyd.
slide: go by, pass.
Sessa: give over, cease.
6 *burst*: broken.
7 *denier*: a worthless French coin.
Go . . . Jeronimy: A misquotation from *The Spanish Tragedy*, where Hieronimo (whose name is now confused with Saint Jerome) warns himself to beware.

SCENE 1

England: outside a country tavern. Enter Christopher Sly *and the* Hostess

Sly
I'll feeze you, in faith.
Hostess
A pair of stocks, you rogue!
Sly
Y'are a baggage, the Slys are no rogues. Look in the Chronicles; we came in with Richard Conqueror.
5 Therefore *paucas pallabris*, let the world slide. Sessa!
Hostess
You will not pay for the glasses you have burst?
Sly
No, not a denier. Go by, Saint Jeronimy, go to thy cold bed and warm thee.

He lies down

Hostess
I know my remedy; I must go fetch the thirdborough.
[Exit
Sly
10 Third, or fourth, or fifth borough, I'll answer him by law. I'll not budge an inch, boy. Let him come, and kindly.

He falls asleep

Wind horns. Enter a Lord *from hunting, with his train of* Huntsmen *and* Servingmen

Lord
Huntsman, I charge thee, tender well my hounds.
Breathe Merriman—the poor cur is emboss'd—
And couple Clowder with the deep-mouth'd brach.

9 *thirdborough*: constable (probably a
   Warwickshire term).
10 *by law*: according to the law.
11 *boy*: A contemptuous form of address.
   kindly: welcome.
11s.d. *Wind*: blow.
12 *charge*: order.
   tender well: take good care of.
13 *Breathe*: give a breathing-space to.
   emboss'd: foaming at the mouth.
14 *couple*: leash together.
   deep-mouth'd brach: bitch with the
   deep voice; the Elizabethans took care
   in matching the voices of their hounds
   to sound in harmony together.

15 *make it good*: picked up the scent.
16 *in . . . fault*: when the scent was least.

19 *cried . . . loss*: discovered the scent
   and cried out when it seemed
   completely lost.

22 *fleet*: fast.

31 *Grim . . . image*: This comparison
   occurs frequently in Shakespeare's
   plays; compare Macbeth, *2*, 3, 72–4:
   'Malcolm, awake, Shake off this
   downy sleep, death's counterfeit, And
   look on death itself'.

15 Saw'st thou not, boy, how Silver made it good
   At the hedge corner, in the coldest fault?
   I would not lose the dog for twenty pound.
      First Huntsman
   Why, Belman is as good as he, my lord;
   He cried upon it at the merest loss,
20 And twice today pick'd out the dullest scent.
   Trust me, I take him for the better dog.
      Lord
   Thou art a fool. If Echo were as fleet
   I would esteem him worth a dozen such.
   But sup them well, and look unto them all:
25 Tomorrow I intend to hunt again.
      First Huntsman
   I will, my lord.
      Lord
   What's here? One dead, or drunk? See, doth he
   breathe?
      Second Huntsman
   He breathes, my lord. Were he not warm'd with ale,
   This were a bed but cold to sleep so soundly.
      Lord
30 O monstrous beast, how like a swine he lies!
   Grim death, how foul and loathsome is thine image!

32 *practise*: play a practical joke.
34 *sweet*: scented.

35 *banquet*: a selection of sweet dishes with fruit and wine.
36 *brave*: finely-dressed.
37 *himself*: his real identity.

38 *choose*: do anything else.

43 *wanton pictures*: The Lord probably means tapestry wall-hangings, depicting amorous scenes.
44 *Balm*: bathe.
distilled waters: distillèd; e.g. rose-water, made from distilled rose petals.
45 *sweet wood*: e.g. juniper, or pine cones.
47 *dulcet*: melodious.
48 *chance*: happens.
straight: immediately.
49 *reverence*: bow.

53 *ewer*: jug.
diaper: towel, napkin.

58 *disease*: (mental) disorder.
59 *lunatic*: deranged, under the influence of the moon (Latin *luna*).
60 *when . . . is*: when he says that he must be mad now.
62 *kindly*: convincingly.
63 *passing*: extremely.
64 *husbanded*: taken care of.
with modesty: properly, without overdoing things.

Sirs, I will practise on this drunken man.
What think you, if he were convey'd to bed,
Wrapp'd in sweet clothes, rings put upon his fingers,
35 A most delicious banquet by his bed,
And brave attendants near him when he wakes—
Would not the beggar then forget himself?
      First Huntsman
Believe me, lord, I think he cannot choose.
      Second Huntsman
It would seem strange unto him when he wak'd—
      Lord
40 Even as a flatt'ring dream or worthless fancy.
Then take him up, and manage well the jest.
Carry him gently to my fairest chamber
And hang it round with all my wanton pictures;
Balm his foul head in warm distilled waters
45 And burn sweet wood to make the lodging sweet;
Procure me music ready when he wakes
To make a dulcet and a heavenly sound;
And if he chance to speak, be ready straight
And with a low submissive reverence
50 Say, 'What is it your honour will command?'
Let one attend him with a silver basin
Full of rose-water and bestrew'd with flowers;
Another bear the ewer, the third a diaper,
And say, 'Will't please your lordship cool your hands?'
55 Some one be ready with a costly suit
And ask him what apparel he will wear;
Another tell him of his hounds and horse,
And that his lady mourns at his disease.
Persuade him that he hath been lunatic,
60 And when he says he is, say that he dreams,
For he is nothing but a mighty lord.
This do, and do it kindly, gentle sirs.
It will be pastime passing excellent,
If it be husbanded with modesty.
      First Huntsman
65 My lord, I warrant you we will play our part
As he shall think by our true diligence
He is no less than what we say he is.

69 *office*: appointed task.

Lord
Take him up gently and to bed with him,
And each one to his office when he wakes.

[Sly *is carried off*

Sound trumpets

70 Sirrah, go see what trumpet 'tis that sounds.

[*Exit* Servingman

Belike some noble gentleman that means,
Travelling some journey, to repose him here.

Enter Servingman

How now? Who is it?
Servingman
                              An't please your honour, players
That offer service to your lordship.

73 *An't*: if it.
73–4 *players . . . lordship*: Acting
   companies were often forced to tour
   the provinces, performing in the halls
   of great houses and in inn yards, when
   the London theatres were closed by
   outbreaks of plague.

Lord
75 Bid them come near.

Enter Players

Now, fellows, you are welcome.
Players
We thank your honour.
Lord
Do you intend to stay with me tonight?
First Player
So please your lordship to accept our duty.
Lord
With all my heart. This fellow I remember

80 Since once he play'd a farmer's eldest son—
'Twas where you wooed the gentlewoman so well—
I have forgot your name, but sure that part
Was aptly fitted and naturally perform'd.
Second Player
I think 'twas Soto that your honour means.
Lord

85 'Tis very true; thou didst it excellent.
Well, you are come to me in happy time,
The rather for I have some sport in hand
Wherein your cunning can assist me much.
There is a lord will hear you play tonight—

90 But I am doubtful of your modesties,
Lest over-eyeing of his odd behaviour
(For yet his honour never heard a play)
You break into some merry passion
And so offend him; for I tell you, sirs,

95 If you should smile, he grows impatient.
First Player
Fear not, my lord, we can contain ourselves
Were he the veriest antic in the world.
Lord
Go, sirrah, take them to the buttery
And give them friendly welcome every one.

100 Let them want nothing that my house affords.
                              [*Exit one with the* Players
Sirrah, go you to Barthol'mew my page
And see him dress'd in all suits like a lady.
That done, conduct him to the drunkard's chamber,
And call him 'madam', do him obeisance.

78 *So please*: if it please.

80 *Since once*: since the time that.

83 *aptly fitted*: well suited.

84 *Soto*: No extant play of this period has a character named Soto, but it is possible that a play now lost was revised by John Fletcher about 1620 with the title *Women Pleased*.
86 *in happy time*: just at the right time.
87 *The rather*: because.
88 *cunning*: skill.

90 *modesties*: self-control.
91 *over-eyeing of*: staring at.
92 *yet . . . play*: he has never seen a play before.
93 *break . . . passion*: start laughing.

97 *veriest*: greatest.
    antic: eccentric.

98 *buttery*: pantry, storeroom.

100 *want*: lack.
    affords: can offer.

101–2 *go . . . lady*: In the Elizabethan theatre, the woman's part was always played by a boy.
102 *suits*: respects (with a pun on 'clothes').

105 *as he will*: if he wants to.
106 *bear . . . action*: behave in a dignified manner.

108 *accomplished*: accomplishèd; performed.

110 *low tongue*: soft voice.
lowly courtesy: humble curtsy.

113 *make known*: demonstrate.
114 *embracements*: embraces.
115 *declining*: lowered.

118 *esteemed him*: esteemèd; thought himself to be.

121 *commanded tears*: tears on command.
122 *do well . . . shift*: be effective for that job.
123 *close convey'd*: secretly carried.
124 *in despite*: unnaturally.

126 *Anon*: in a minute.

127 *usurp*: imitate.
128 *gait, and action*: walk and bodily movement.

130 *stay*: restrain.
131 *simple*: foolish.
132 *I'll . . . them*: I'll go inside to warn them.
Haply: perhaps.
133 *abate*: moderate.
over-merry spleen: excessive merriment; the spleen was believed to be the seat of most strong emotions.

105 Tell him from me—as he will win my love—
He bear himself with honourable action
Such as he hath observ'd in noble ladies
Unto their lords, by them accomplished.
Such duty to the drunkard let him do
110 With soft low tongue and lowly courtesy,
And say, 'What is't your honour will command
Wherein your lady and your humble wife
May show her duty and make known her love?'
And then with kind embracements, tempting kisses,
115 And with declining head into his bosom,
Bid him shed tears, as being overjoy'd
To see her noble lord restor'd to health,
Who for this seven years hath esteemed him
No better than a poor and loathsome beggar.
120 And if the boy have not a woman's gift
To rain a shower of commanded tears,
An onion will do well for such a shift,
Which in a napkin being close convey'd
Shall in despite enforce a watery eye.
125 See this dispatch'd with all the haste thou canst;
Anon I'll give thee more instructions.

[Exit a Servingman

I know the boy will well usurp the grace,
Voice, gait, and action of a gentlewoman.
I long to hear him call the drunkard 'husband',
130 And how my men will stay themselves from laughter
When they do homage to this simple peasant.
I'll in to counsel them. Haply my presence
May well abate the over-merry spleen
Which otherwise would grow into extremes.

[Exeunt

Induction Scene 2
Two life-styles are contrasted when the
nobleman's servants persuade Sly that he is
indeed a gentleman.

Os.d. *aloft*: The scene probably begins
    on the balcony above the stage, but
    there would not be enough space for
    the characters to remain above for the
    entire scene.
1 *small ale*: the weakest (and cheapest)
    beer. At the beginning of the scene
    Sly speaks in prose, and asks for 'ale':
    the courtly servingmen answer in
    verse, and offer him 'sack'.
2 *sack*: dry white wine.
3 *conserves*: fruit preserved in sugar.

4 *raiment*: clothing.

5 *Christophero*: Sly attempts to assert
    himself with a Spanish version of his
    name.
7 *conserves of beef*: beef preserved in
    salt.
8 *doublets*: jackets, close-fitting tunics.

11 *overleather*: upper part of the shoe.

SCENE 2

The Lord'*s house: enter aloft* Sly *with* Attendants—
some with apparel, basin, and ewer, and other
appurtenances—and Lord

Sly
For God's sake, a pot of small ale!
    First Servingman
Will't please your lordship drink a cup of sack!
    Second Servingman
Will't please your honour taste of these conserves?
    Third Servingman
What raiment will your honour wear today?
    Sly
5 I am Christophero Sly—call not me 'honour' nor
'lordship'. I ne'er drank sack in my life, and if you give
me any conserves, give me conserves of beef. Ne'er ask
me what raiment I'll wear, for I have no more doublets
than backs, no more stockings than legs, nor no more
10 shoes than feet—nay, sometime more feet than shoes,
or such shoes as my toes look through the overleather.

12 *idle humour*: foolish mood.
13 *descent*: noble birth.
14 *esteem*: reputation.
15 *infused*: infusèd; possessed.
16 *would you*: do you want to.
17–20 *Burton-heath . . . Wincot*: Villages near Stratford-upon-Avon, Shakespeare's birthplace; a family called Hacket was living in Wincot in 1591.
18 *cardmaker*: maker of 'cards'—toothed instruments for combing wool. *transmutation*: changing his job. *bear-herd*: keeper of a performing bear.
20 *ale-wife*: woman who keeps an ale-house.
21 *on the score*: in debt; alehouse debts were chalked up on a slate.
21–2 *sheer ale*: just for ale.
22 *score*: mark. *Christendom*: the Christian world.
23 *bestraught*: mad, out of my mind. *Here's—*: Sly is trying to offer proof of his identity, but he can find none.

27 *As*: as though.

29 *ancient*: former.

32 *beck*: nod.
33 *Apollo*: the classical god of music.
34 *caged*: cagèd.

36 *lustful*: enticing.
37 *trimm'd up*: dressed up. *Semiramis*: a legendary queen of Assyria, renowned for amorous encounters.
38 *bestrow*: spread rushes (probably) as a carpet.
39 *trapp'd*: draped in decorative coverings.
43 *welkin*: sky—a 'poetic' word.

45 *course*: hunt the hare.
46 *breathed*: breathèd; strong-winded. *fleeter . . . roe*: swifter than the deer.

Lord
Heaven cease this idle humour in your honour!
O that a mighty man of such descent,
Of such possessions and so high esteem,
15 Should be infused with so foul a spirit!
    Sly
What, would you make me mad? Am not I Christopher
Sly, old Sly's son of Burton-heath, by birth a pedlar, by
education a cardmaker, by transmutation a bear-herd,
and now by present profession a tinker? Ask Marian
20 Hacket, the fat ale-wife of Wincot, if she know me not.
If she say I am not fourteen pence on the score for sheer
ale, score me up for the lying'st knave in Christendom.
What, I am not bestraught! Here's—
    Third Servingman
O, this it is that makes your lady mourn.
    Second Servingman
25 O, this is it that makes your servants droop.
    Lord
Hence comes it that your kindred shuns your house
As beaten hence by your strange lunacy.
O noble lord, bethink thee of thy birth.
Call home thy ancient thoughts from banishment,
30 And banish hence these abject lowly dreams.
Look how thy servants do attend on thee,
Each in his office ready at thy beck.
Wilt thou have music? Hark, Apollo plays,   [*Music*]
And twenty caged nightingales do sing.
35 Or wilt thou sleep? We'll have thee to a couch
Softer and sweeter than the lustful bed
On purpose trimm'd up for Semiramis.
Say thou wilt walk, we will bestrow the ground.
Or wilt thou ride? Thy horses shall be trapp'd,
40 Their harness studded all with gold and pearl.
Dost thou love hawking? Thou hast hawks will soar
Above the morning lark. Or wilt thou hunt?
Thy hounds shall make the welkin answer them
And fetch shrill echoes from the hollow earth.
    First Servingman
45 Say thou wilt course, thy greyhounds are as swift
As breathed stags, ay, fleeter than the roe.

47 *straight*: immediately.

48–58 *Adonis . . . drawn*: Illustrations of erotic moments in Ovid's *Metamorphoses*. Venus ('Cytherea'), the goddess of love, tried to seduce Adonis, a handsome human boy; Shakespeare tells the story in his poem *Venus and Adonis*. Io was raped by the god Zeus, hidden in a mist, and turned into a heifer; Daphne escaped from the clutches of Apollo when she was changed into a laurel tree.

49 *sedges*: rushes.

53 *beguiled*: beguilèd.

54 *lively*: lifelike.
as . . . done: as when the act was performed.

58 *workmanly*: skilfully.

60 *Thou . . . lady*: The descriptions of erotic pictures have been leading up to this climax.

61 *this waning age*: this decaying modern world (which was thought to be declining from the perfection of the classical Golden Age).

62 *till*: before, until.

63 *envious*: malicious.
o'er-run: flowed over.

65 *yet*: even so.

66–73 *Am I . . . ale*: Sly, persuaded that he is indeed a lord, begins to speak in verse; he checks out his five senses for confirmation—but betrays himself when he calls for the cheapest beer.

75 *wit*: intelligence, sanity.

77 *fifteen*: The servingman increases the Lord's time.

Second Servingman
Dost thou love pictures? We will fetch thee straight
Adonis painted by a running brook,
And Cytherea all in sedges hid,
50 Which seem to move and wanton with her breath
Even as the waving sedges play wi'th'wind.
　Lord
We'll show thee Io as she was a maid,
And how she was beguiled and surpris'd,
As lively painted as the deed was done.
　Third Servingman
55 Or Daphne roaming through a thorny wood,
Scratching her legs that one shall swear she bleeds,
And at that sight shall sad Apollo weep,
So workmanly the blood and tears are drawn.
　Lord
Thou art a lord, and nothing but a lord.
60 Thou hast a lady far more beautiful
Than any woman in this waning age.
　First Servingman
And till the tears that she hath shed for thee
Like envious floods o'er-run her lovely face,
She was the fairest creature in the world—
65 And yet she is inferior to none.
　Sly
Am I a lord, and have I such a lady?
Or do I dream? Or have I dream'd till now?
I do not sleep: I see, I hear, I speak,
I smell sweet savours and I feel soft things.
70 Upon my life, I am a lord indeed,
And not a tinker, nor Christopher Sly.
Well, bring our lady hither to our sight,
And once again a pot o'th'smallest ale.
　　　　　　　　　　[*Exit a* Servingman
　Second Servingman
Will't please your mightiness to wash your hands?
75 O, how we joy to see your wit restor'd!
O, that once more you knew but what you are!
These fifteen years you have been in a dream,
Or when you wak'd, so wak'd as if you slept.

79 *fay*: faith.

80 *of*: during.

81 *idle*: silly.
82 *goodly*: fine.
83 *out of door*: out of the house.
84 *rail upon*: shout about.
85 *leet*: small local court.
86 *seal'd quarts*: The quart (= ½ litre) measures were officially stamped to guarantee capacity—but unscrupulous innkeepers sometimes used deceptive earthenware jugs.
87 *Cicely Hacket*: see note to lines 17–20.
88 *the . . . house*: the landlady's daughter.
90 *reckon'd up*: referred to.
91 *Greece*: This may be a misreading of 'Greet', the name of another village near Stratford.

95 *thanked*: thankèd.
    amends: improvement.

97 *I thank thee*: Sly acknowledges the drink he has been given.
    thou . . . it: i.e. I'll pay you later.
98 *How fares*: how is. The page is enquiring about the 'lord's' health; but Sly in the next line makes a pun on 'fare' = take nourishment.
99 *cheer*: nourishment.

103 *goodman*: The peasant's word for 'husband'.

Sly
These fifteen years! By my fay, a goodly nap.
80 But did I never speak of all that time?
    First Servingman
O yes, my lord, but very idle words,
For though you lay here in this goodly chamber,
Yet would you say ye were beaten out of door,
And rail upon the hostess of the house,
85 And say you would present her at the leet
Because she brought stone jugs and no seal'd quarts.
Sometimes you would call out for Cicely Hacket.
    Sly
Ay, the woman's maid of the house.
    Third Servingman
Why, sir, you know no house, nor no such maid,
90 Nor no such men as you have reckon'd up,
As Stephen Sly and old John Naps of Greece,
And Peter Turph and Henry Pimpernell,
And twenty more such names and men as these,
Which never were, nor no man ever saw.
    Sly
95 Now Lord be thanked for my good amends!
    All
Amen.

Enter Bartholomew, *a page, dressed as a lady, with*
Attendants, *one of whom gives* Sly *a pot of ale*

    Sly
I thank thee, thou shalt not lose by it.
    Bartholomew
How fares my noble lord?
    Sly
Marry, I fare well, for here is cheer enough. [*He drinks*]
100 Where is my wife?
    Bartholomew
Here, noble lord, what is thy will with her?
    Sly
Are you my wife, and will not call me 'husband'?
My men should call me 'lord'; I am your goodman.

Bartholomew

My husband and my lord, my lord and husband,

105 I am your wife in all obedience.

Sly

I know it well—What must I call her?

Lord

'Madam'.

Sly

'Al'ce madam' or 'Joan madam'?

Lord

'Madam' and nothing else. So lords call ladies.

Sly

110 Madam wife, they say that I have dream'd

And slept above some fifteen year or more.

Bartholomew

Ay, and the time seems thirty unto me,

Being all this time abandon'd from your bed.

Sly

'Tis much. Servants, leave me and her alone.

[*Exeunt* Servingmen

115 Madam, undress you and come now to bed.

Bartholomew

Thrice noble lord, let me entreat of you

To pardon me yet for a night or two,

Or, if not so, until the sun be set.

For your physicians have expressly charg'd,

120 In peril to incur your former malady,

That I should yet absent me from your bed.

I hope this reason stands for my excuse.

Sly

Ay, it stands so that I may hardly tarry so long, but I would be loath to fall into my dreams again. I will

125 therefore tarry in despite of the flesh and the blood.

Enter a Messenger

Messenger

Your honour's players, hearing your amendment,

Are come to play a pleasant comedy;

For so your doctors hold it very meet,

Seeing too much sadness hath congeal'd your blood

---

105 *in all obedience*: In the old form of the Marriage Service, the woman promised to 'love, honour, and obey' her husband.

113 *abandon'd*: banished.

117 *pardon*: excuse.

119 *expressly charg'd*: especially ordered.
120 *In peril*: at the risk of.

123 *it stands*: Sly is aroused—and forgets the formal verse in his sexual innuendoes.
hardly: with difficulty.
tarry: hold back, wait.

128 *hold it very meet*: think it is a very good idea.
129–30 *Seeing . . . frenzy*: Melancholy was thought to be caused by a thickening of the blood, and to be itself the cause ('nurse') of madness.

132 *frame*: suit.

133 *bars*: prevents.

134 *comonty*: The word 'comedy' is new to Sly.

135 *gambold*: game.
tumbling trick: acrobatics.

137 *household stuff*: homely fun.

138 *history*: story, narrative.

141 *And . . . younger*: Sly speaks the verse line of a gentleman as he prepares to enjoy this new entertainment.

130 And melancholy is the nurse of frenzy—
Therefore they thought it good to hear a play
And frame your mind to mirth and merriment,
Which bars a thousand harms and lengthens life.
    Sly
Marry, I will. Let them play it. Is not a comonty a
135 Christmas gambold or a tumbling trick?
    Bartholomew
No, my good lord, it is more pleasing stuff.
    Sly
What, household stuff?
    Bartholomew
It is a kind of history.
    Sly
Well, we'll see't.   [*Exit* Messenger
140 Come, madam wife, sit by my side,
And let the world slip. We shall ne'er be younger.

    They sit down

    A flourish of trumpets to announce the play

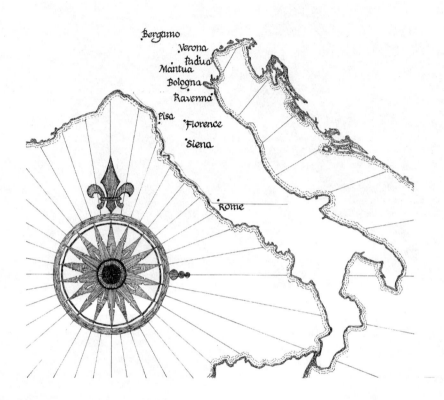

Bergamo
Verona
Padua
Mantua
Bologna
Ravenna
Pisa
Florence
Siena
Rome

Act 1 Scene 1

The play proper begins. Lucentio, newly
arrived in Padua, overhears a family
quarrel. Baptista refuses to consider the
suitors for his younger daughter Bianca
until he finds a husband for her sister
Katherina. Lucentio, already in love with
Bianca, exchanges clothes with his servant
Tranio so that he can court her in disguise.

1 *since for*: because of.
2 *Padua*: Padua was famous for its
   ancient university (founded 1228).
   arts: learning.

SCENE 1

Padua: a street. Enter Lucentio *and his man* Tranio

Lucentio
Tranio, since for the great desire I had
To see fair Padua, nursery of arts,
I am arriv'd for fruitful Lombardy,
The pleasant garden of great Italy,
5 And by my father's love and leave am arm'd

'Here let us breathe and haply institute A course of learning . . . ' (*1*, 1, 8–9). Dermot Kerrigan as Lucentio and Mark Lockyer as Tranio, Royal Shakespeare Company, 1995.

3 *am arriv'd for*: have arrived in.
3–4 *fruitful . . . Italy*: The description derives from John Florio's manual for the study of Italian ('*La Lombardia è il giardino del mondo*').
5 *leave*: permission.
7 *well approv'd in all*: shown by experience to be good in every way.
8 *breathe*: pause, have a rest.
   haply: maybe.
   institute: begin.
9 *ingenuous*: liberal, suitable for a gentleman.
10 *Pisa . . . citizens*: The line, repeated at *4, 2, 95*, was perhaps some kind of catchphrase.
   renowned: renownèd; famous.
11 *first*: before me.
12 *great . . . world*: major international enterprises.
13 *come of*: descended from.
   the Bentivolii: a great Italian family (actually from Bologna, not Pisa).
14–16 *Vincentio's son . . . deeds*: it is only right that Vincentio's son, brought up in Florence, should fulfil all expectations by adorning his good fortunes with noble actions.
19 *apply*: concentrate on.
19–20 *that . . . achiev'd*: Aristotle's *Ethics* deals with ('treats of') the notion that true happiness can only be achieved through virtuous living.
21 *thy mind*: what you think of it.
22 *as he that*: like someone who.
23 *plash*: puddle.
24 *satiety*: over-indulgence.
25 *Mi perdonato*: pardon me; such Italian phrases (from Florio's manual) are intended to persuade the audience that the action has moved away from rural Warwickshire.
26 *affected*: disposed.
27 *resolve*: determination.
28 *suck the sweets*: imbibe the nectar (like a bee).
31 *stoics . . . stocks*: Tranio makes a common pun: 'stoics' endure everything, and 'stocks' appreciate nothing.
32 *checks*: disciplines.
33 *As . . . abjur'd*: that Ovid (and his erotic poetry) is completely thrown out.
34–7 *Balk . . . metaphysics*: Tranio refers to the subjects of the university syllabus.

With his good will and thy good company—
My trusty servant well approv'd in all—
Here let us breathe and haply institute
A course of learning and ingenuous studies.
10 Pisa renowned for grave citizens
Gave me my being and my father first,
A merchant of great traffic through the world,
Vincentio, come of the Bentivolii.
Vincentio's son, brought up in Florence,
15 It shall become to serve all hopes conceiv'd
To deck his fortune with his virtuous deeds.
And therefore, Tranio, for the time I study,
Virtue and that part of philosophy
Will I apply that treats of happiness
20 By virtue specially to be achiev'd.
Tell me thy mind, for I have Pisa left
And am to Padua come as he that leaves
A shallow plash to plunge him in the deep
And with satiety seeks to quench his thirst.
    Tranio
25 *Mi perdonato*, gentle master mine,
I am in all affected as yourself,
Glad that you thus continue your resolve
To suck the sweets of sweet philosophy.
Only, good master, while we do admire
30 This virtue and this moral discipline,
Let's be no stoics nor no stocks, I pray,
Or so devote to Aristotle's checks
As Ovid be an outcast quite abjur'd.
Balk logic with acquaintance that you have
35 And practise rhetoric in your common talk;
Music and poesy use to quicken you;
The mathematics and the metaphysics—
Fall to them as you find your stomach serves you.
No profit grows where is no pleasure tane:
40 In brief, sir, study what you most affect.
    Lucentio
Gramercies, Tranio, well dost thou advise.
If, Biondello, thou wert come ashore,
We could at once put us in readiness

34 *Balk logic*: engage in formal
    arguments.
    acquaintance: friends.
35 *rhetoric*: the art of communication.
36 *quicken*: enliven, entertain.
38 *stomach*: appetite, taste.
39 *tane*: taken.
40 *most affect*: like best.
41 *Gramercies*: many thanks.
42 *come ashore*: Padua and the cities of
    Northern Italy are linked by a network
    of inland waterways.
43 *put . . . readiness*: get started.
45s.d. *pantaloon*: foolish old man; a
    stock figure in the Italian *commedia
    dell'arte*, whose role was usually to
    serve as an obstacle to the young
    lovers.
47 *show*: pageant, entertainment.

48 *importune . . . farther*: don't go on
    asking me.

50 *bestow*: give (in marriage).
    youngest: younger.

54 *Leave*: permission.

55 *cart her*: treat her (with a pun on
    'court her') like a prostitute (who were
    whipped as they were drawn through
    the streets behind a cart).

58 *stale*: a) laughing stock; b) prostitute.
    mates: crude fellows.

60 *mould*: nature.

62 *Iwis*: indeed.

64 *comb your noddle*: hit you over your
    silly head.
65 *paint*: i.e. with blood.

66 *From . . . us*: Hortensio quotes a
    traditional protective incantation:
    'From the crafts and assaults of the
    devil . . . Good Lord, deliver us'.

And take a lodging fit to entertain
45 Such friends as time in Padua shall beget.

> *Enter* Baptista *with his two daughters,* Katherina *and*
> Bianca; Gremio, *a pantaloon, and* Hortensio, *suitor*
> *to* Bianca

But stay awhile, what company is this?
Tranio
Master, some show to welcome us to town.

> Lucentio *and* Tranio *stand by*

Baptista
Gentlemen, importune me no farther
For how I firmly am resolv'd you know—
50 That is, not to bestow my youngest daughter
Before I have a husband for the elder.
If either of you both love Katherina,
Because I know you well and love you well,
Leave shall you have to court her at your pleasure.
Gremio
55 To cart her rather! She's too rough for me.
There, there, Hortensio, will you any wife?
Katherina
[*To* Baptista] I pray you, sir, is it your will
To make a stale of me amongst these mates?
Hortensio
'Mates', maid? How mean you that? No mates for you
60 Unless you were of gentler, milder mould.
Katherina
I'faith, sir, you shall never need to fear.
Iwis it is not halfway to her heart—
But if it were, doubt not her care should be
To comb your noddle with a three-legg'd stool
65 And paint your face and use you like a fool.
Hortensio
From all such devils, good Lord deliver us!
Gremio
And me too, good Lord!

68 *toward*: about to happen.
69 *froward*: bad-tempered.

71 *sobriety*: modesty.

73 *Mum*: keep quiet.

74 *make good*: accomplish.

78 *peat*: little pet.
It is best: you ought to.
finger in the eye: i.e. to bring tears.
78–9 *and . . . why*: if she had any sense.
80 *content . . . discontent*: be satisfied now that I am unhappy.
81 *pleasure*: will.
subscribe: obey.

84 *Minerva*: the Roman goddess of wisdom.

85 *strange*: unfriendly.
86 *effects*: causes.

87 *mew*: cage (like a hawk during its moulting—'mewing'—period).

89 *make . . . tongue*: make Bianca pay for what Katherina says.

90 *content ye*: you must be satisfied.
am resolv'd: have made my mind up.

Tranio
[*Aside to* Lucentio] Husht, master, here's some good
    pastime toward;
That wench is stark mad, or wonderful froward.
    Lucentio
70 [*Aside to* Tranio] But in the other's silence do I see
Maid's mild behaviour and sobriety.
Peace, Tranio.
    Tranio
[*Aside to* Lucentio] Well said, master. Mum! And gaze
    your fill.
    Baptista
Gentlemen, that I may soon make good
75 What I have said—Bianca, get you in.
And let it not displease thee, good Bianca,
For I will love thee ne'er the less, my girl.
    Katherina
A pretty peat! It is best put finger in the eye, and she
knew why.
    Bianca
80 Sister, content you in my discontent.
Sir, to your pleasure humbly I subscribe.
My books and instruments shall be my company,
On them to look and practise by myself.
    Lucentio
[*Aside*] Hark, Tranio, thou mayst hear Minerva speak!
    Hortensio
85 Signor Baptista, will you be so strange?
Sorry am I that our good will effects
Bianca's grief.
    Gremio
                    Why will you mew her up,
Signor Baptista, for this fiend of hell,
And make her bear the penance of her tongue?
    Baptista
90 Gentlemen, content ye. I am resolv'd.
Go in, Bianca.   [*Exit* Bianca
And, for I know she taketh most delight
In music, instruments, and poetry,
Schoolmasters will I keep within my house
95 Fit to instruct her youth. If you, Hortensio,

97   *Prefer them hither*: introduce me to
      them.
      cunning: skilful.
98   *liberal*: generous.
99   *bringing up*: education.

101   *commune*: discuss.

105   *dam*: mother (the archetypal shrew).
      gifts: qualities, abilities.
106–8 *Love . . . sides*: love isn't so
      important but we can wait patiently
      and survive without it; it's the same
      for both of us. Gremio and Hortensio
      converse in a string of commonplaces.
110   *light on*: find.
111   *wish*: recommend.

113   *brooked parle*: allowed us to talk to
      each other.
114   *upon advice*: on consideration.
      toucheth: concerns.

119   *Marry*: by (the Virgin) Mary (a mild
      oath).

123   *so very a fool*: such a complete fool.

126   *alarums*: war-cries (literally, the
      trumpet-calls to battle).

Or Signor Gremio you, know any such,
Prefer them hither; for to cunning men
I will be very kind, and liberal
To mine own children in good bringing up.
100 And so farewell. Katherina, you may stay,
For I have more to commune with Bianca.   [*Exit*
       Katherina
Why, and I trust I may go too, may I not?
What, shall I be appointed hours as though, belike,
I knew not what to take and what to leave? Ha!   [*Exit*
       Gremio
105 You may go to the devil's dam! Your gifts are so good
here's none will hold you. There! Love is not so great,
Hortensio, but we may blow our nails together and fast
it fairly out. Our cake's dough on both sides. Farewell.
Yet, for the love I bear my sweet Bianca, if I can by any
110 means light on a fit man to teach her that wherein she
delights, I will wish him to her father.
       Hortensio
So will I, Signor Gremio. But a word, I pray. Though the
nature of our quarrel yet never brooked parle, know
now, upon advice, it toucheth us both—that we may yet
115 again have access to our fair mistress and be happy
rivals in Bianca's love—to labour and effect one thing
specially.
       Gremio
What's that, I pray?
       Hortensio
Marry, sir, to get a husband for her sister.
       Gremio
120 A husband? A devil!
       Hortensio
I say a husband.
       Gremio
I say a devil. Think'st thou, Hortensio, though her father
be very rich, any man is so very a fool to be married to
hell?
       Hortensio
125 Tush, Gremio. Though it pass your patience and mine
to endure her loud alarums—why, man, there be good

fellows in the world, and a man could light on them, would take her with all faults, and money enough.

Gremio

I cannot tell. But I had as lief take her dowry with this
130 condition: to be whipped at the high cross every morning.

Hortensio

Faith, as you say, there's small choice in rotten apples. But come, since this bar in law makes us friends, it shall be so far forth friendly maintained till by helping
135 Baptista's eldest daughter to a husband we set his youngest free for a husband—and then have to't afresh. Sweet Bianca! Happy man be his dole! He that runs fastest gets the ring. How say you, Signor Gremio?

Gremio

I am agreed, and would I had given him the best horse
140 in Padua to begin his wooing that would thoroughly woo her, wed her, and bed her, and rid the house of her. Come on.   [*Exeunt* Gremio *and* Hortensio

Tranio

I pray sir, tell me, is it possible
That love should of a sudden take such hold?

Lucentio

145 O Tranio, till I found it to be true
I never thought it possible or likely.
But see! while idly I stood looking on,
I found the effect of love-in-idleness,
And now in plainness do confess to thee
150 That art to me as secret and as dear
As Anna to the Queen of Carthage was—

129 *I cannot tell*: I don't know about that.
    as lief: just as soon.
130 *high cross*: market cross (at town centre).

132 *small choice in*: little difference between.
133 *bar in law*: legal obstacle (i.e. Baptista's declaration).
134 *friendly maintained*: kept up in a friendly manner.
136 *have to't afresh*: on with the battle.
137 *Happy . . . dole*: let the winner be happy.
137–8 *He . . . ring*: The metaphor is sporting—with obscene implications.

139 *him*: any man.

148 *love-in-idleness*: the pansy; Lucentio alludes to the flower's supposed aphrodisiac power.
149 *plainness*: honesty.
150 *secret*: trustworthy.
151 *Anna*: the sister-in-law and confidante of Dido in Virgil's *Aeneid* (Book 4); their tragic deaths by burning were dramatized by Christopher Marlowe in *The Tragedy of Dido, Queen of Carthage*.

153 *achieve*: win.

157 *rated*: driven.

159 *Redime . . . minimo*: ransom yourself,
    now that you have been captured, for
    as little as possible; the quotation
    (from a comedy by Terence) appears
    in Lyly's *Latin Grammar*, the textbook
    used in most Elizabethan schools.
160 *Gramercies*: many thanks.

163 *you . . . all*: you didn't see what was
    the real issue; it was often necessary,
    in classical comedy, for the servant to
    explain the plot to his master.
165 *daughter of Agenor*: Europa; Jove
    transformed himself into a bull and
    carried her away to Crete.

170 *hardly*: scarcely.

177 *curst and shrewd*: bad-tempered and
    perverse.

180 *mew'd*: confined (see line 87 note).
181 *Because*: in order that.

183 *art . . . advis'd*: didn't you notice.
184 *cunning*: skilful.

Tranio, I burn! I pine, I perish, Tranio,
If I achieve not this young modest girl.
Counsel me, Tranio, for I know thou canst;
155 Assist me, Tranio, for I know thou wilt.
       Tranio
Master, it is no time to chide you now;
Affection is not rated from the heart.
If love have touched you, naught remains but so:
Redime te captum quam queas minimo.
       Lucentio
160 Gramercies, lad. Go forward. This contents;
The rest will comfort, for thy counsel's sound.
       Tranio
Master, you look'd so longly on the maid,
Perhaps you mark'd not what's the pith of all.
       Lucentio
O yes, I saw sweet beauty in her face,
165 Such as the daughter of Agenor had,
That made great Jove to humble him to her hand
When with his knees he kiss'd the Cretan strand.
       Tranio
Saw you no more? Mark'd you not how her sister
Began to scold and raise up such a storm
170 That mortal ears might hardly endure the din?
       Lucentio
Tranio, I saw her coral lips to move,
And with her breath she did perfume the air.
Sacred and sweet was all I saw in her.
       Tranio
Nay, then, 'tis time to stir him from his trance.
175 I pray, awake, sir. If you love the maid
Bend thoughts and wits to achieve her. Thus it stands:
Her elder sister is so curst and shrewd
That, till the father rid his hands of her,
Master, your love must live a maid at home,
180 And therefore has he closely mew'd her up,
Because she will not be annoy'd with suitors.
       Lucentio
Ah, Tranio, what a cruel father's he!
But art thou not advis'd he took some care
To get her cunning schoolmasters to instruct her?

185 *'tis plotted*: I have a plan.

186 *for my hand*: at a guess.
187 *inventions*: schemes.
    jump in one: coincide.

190 *device*: plan.
    May it be done: will it work.

191 *bear your part*: take your place.

193 *Keep house*: entertain guests.
    ply his book: pursue his studies.

195 *Basta*: enough (Italian; see line 25 note).
    full: all worked out.

200 *port*: lifestyle.

202 *meaner*: humbler (i.e. than Lucentio himself).

204 *Uncase*: undress.
    colour'd: Elizabethan servants were soberly dressed; the coloured clothes were worn by their masters.

206 *charm*: make him promise.

207 *So . . . need*: it will be necessary.
208 *sith*: since.
209 *tied*: bound.

Tranio
185 Ay, marry, am I, sir—and now 'tis plotted!
      Lucentio
      I have it, Tranio!
            Tranio
                        Master, for my hand,
      Both our inventions meet and jump in one.
            Lucentio
      Tell me thine first.
            Tranio
                        You will be schoolmaster
      And undertake the teaching of the maid—
190 That's your device.
            Lucentio
                        It is. May it be done?
            Tranio
      Not possible. For who shall bear your part
      And be in Padua here Vincentio's son,
      Keep house, and ply his book, welcome his friends,
      Visit his countrymen and banquet them?
            Lucentio
195 *Basta!* Content thee, for I have it full.
      We have not yet been seen in any house,
      Nor can we be distinguish'd by our faces
      For man or master. Then it follows thus:
      Thou shalt be master, Tranio, in my stead;
200 Keep house and port and servants as I should.
      I will some other be—some Florentine,
      Some Neapolitan or meaner man of Pisa.
      'Tis hatch'd and shall be so. Tranio, at once
      Uncase thee; take my colour'd hat and cloak.

      They exchange clothes

205 When Biondello comes, he waits on thee,
      But I will charm him first to keep his tongue.
            Tranio
      So had you need.
      In brief, sir, sith it your pleasure is,
      And I am tied to be obedient—

210 *at our parting*: when we left.
211 *be serviceable*: do your best to serve.

217 *thrall'd*: enslaved.
wounded eye: Cupid's arrow, inducing love, wounded Lucentio in the eye when he saw Bianca.

221 *what's the news*: what's going on.

223 *frame*: fit.

225 *count'nance*: identity.
226–8 *And . . . descried*: Lucentio invents the incident—perhaps to ensure Biondello's silence.
228 *descried*: seen.
229 *as becomes*: in the proper way.

231 *Ne'er a whit*: not at all.

232 *not . . . 'Tranio'*: not a word about Tranio.

235–40 *So . . . Lucentio*: Rhyming couplets mark Tranio's change of identity.

210 For so your father charg'd me at our parting:
'Be serviceable to my son', quoth he,
Although I think 'twas in another sense—
I am content to be Lucentio,
Because so well I love Lucentio.
    Lucentio
215 Tranio, be so, because Lucentio loves,
And let me be a slave t'achieve that maid
Whose sudden sight hath thrall'd my wounded eye.

    Enter Biondello

Here comes the rogue. Sirrah, where have you been?
    Biondello
Where have I been? Nay, how now, where are you?
220 Master, has my fellow Tranio stolen your clothes or you
stolen his, or both? Pray, what's the news?
    Lucentio
Sirrah, come hither. 'Tis no time to jest,
And therefore frame your manners to the time.
Your fellow Tranio here, to save my life,
225 Puts my apparel and my count'nance on,
And I for my escape have put on his;
For in a quarrel since I came ashore
I kill'd a man, and fear I was descried.
Wait you on him, I charge you, as becomes,
230 While I make way from hence to save my life.
You understand me?
    Biondello
                                    Ay, sir. Ne'er a whit.
    Lucentio
And not a jot of 'Tranio' in your mouth:
Tranio is changed into Lucentio.
    Biondello
The better for him! Would I were so too.
    Tranio
235 So could I, faith, boy, to have the next wish after—
That Lucentio indeed had Baptista's youngest
        daughter.
But, sirrah, not for my sake but your master's, I advise

238 *use your manners*: behave yourself.

You use your manners discreetly in all kind of
    companies.
When I am alone, why then I am Tranio,
240 But in all places else your master Lucentio.
    Lucentio
Tranio, let's go.

242 *rests*: remains.
    that thyself execute: which you must
    carry out.
244 *Sufficeth*: let it be enough for you to
    know.

One thing more rests that thyself execute:
To make one among these wooers. If thou ask me why,
Sufficeth my reasons are both good and weighty.
                         [Exeunt

244s.d. *Presenters*: commentators (actors
    playing the parts of spectators).

The Presenters *above speaks*

245 *nod*: fall asleep.
    mind: pay attention to.

    Lord
245 My lord, you nod; you do not mind the play.
    Sly

246 *Saint Anne*: mother of the Virgin Mary.
    matter: subject.

Yes, by Saint Anne, do I. A good matter surely. Comes
there any more of it?
    Bartholomew
My lord, 'tis but begun.
    Sly

250s.d. *sit and mark*: The stage direction
    seems to indicate that the 'Presenters'
    remain in their positions for the rest of
    the play, but Shakespeare seems to
    forget about them: they never speak
    again in *The Taming of the Shrew*. See
    Appendix A, p.114.

'Tis a very excellent piece of work, madam lady. Would
250 'twere done!

    They sit and mark

Act 1 Scene 2
Petruchio has come to Padua to find a rich
wife, and he happily agrees to court
Katherina. Gremio presents Lucentio
(disguised as Tranio) as a teacher for
Bianca, and the real Tranio (calling himself
Lucentio) makes a third suitor for Baptista's
younger daughter.

Scene 2

Padua: outside Hortensio's *house. Enter* Petruchio
and his man Grumio

  2 *of all*: especially.
  3 *beloved*: belovèd.
    approved: approvèd; trusted.
  4 *trow*: believe.
  6–7 *knock . . . worship*: Grumio relies
    on the stock comedy routines of
    Elizabethan clowns—
    misunderstandings and mistaken
    words (malapropisms); 'rebused' =
    'rebuked' and 'abused'.

    Petruchio
Verona, for a while I take my leave
To see my friends in Padua, but of all
My best beloved and approved friend,
Hortensio: and I trow this is his house.
5 Here, sirrah Grumio, knock, I say.
    Grumio
Knock, sir? Whom should I knock? Is there any man has
rebused your worship?

8 *knock me*: knock for me (an archaic
dative form).

11–14 *knock . . . sing it*: The doggerel
rhyming couplets speed up the
slapstick comedy.
12 *knave's pate*: head of a fool.
13–14 *I should . . . worst*: if I hit you first
I know that you will hit me harder in
return.

15 *Will . . . be*: will he never understand.
16 *and*: if.
ring it: ring the bell—with a pun on
'wring'.
17 *sol-fa*: sing a scale of music.

21 *How . . . all*: how is everybody.

22 *fray*: scuffle, fighting.

23 *Con . . . trovato*: with all my heart,
well met.

24–5 *Alla . . . Petruchio*: welcome to our
house, much honoured Signor
Petruchio.
26 *compound*: settle.

27 *ledges*: alleges.
in Latin: Grumio is, momentarily, an
English servant, mistaking Italian for
Latin—and mistrustful of foreign
languages.

Petruchio
Villain, I say, knock me here soundly.
  Grumio
Knock you here, sir? Why, sir, what am I, sir, that I
10 should knock you here, sir?
  Petruchio
Villain, I say, knock me at this gate,
And rap me well, or I'll knock your knave's pate!
  Grumio
My master is grown quarrelsome. I should knock you
    first,
And then I know after who comes by the worst.
  Petruchio
15 Will it not be?
Faith, sirrah, and you'll not knock, I'll ring it.
I'll try how you can *sol-fa*, and sing it.

    He wrings him by the ears

  Grumio
Help, mistress, help! My master is mad.
  Petruchio
Now knock when I bid you, sirrah villain.

    Enter Hortensio

  Hortensio
20 How now, what's the matter? My old friend Grumio and
my good friend Petruchio! How do you all at Verona?
  Petruchio
Signor Hortensio, come you to part the fray?
Con tutto il cuore ben trovato, may I say.
  Hortensio
Alla nostra casa ben venuto
25 *Molto honorato signor mio Petruchio.*
Rise, Grumio, rise. We will compound this quarrel.
  Grumio
Nay, 'tis no matter, sir, what he ledges in Latin. If this be
not a lawful cause for me to leave his service—look you,
sir: he bid me knock him and rap him soundly, sir. Well,

31 *two . . . out*: in error, with something
missing; Grumio alludes to a card
game, 'one and thirty', in which the
player must collect cards whose spots
('pips') add up exactly to 31.

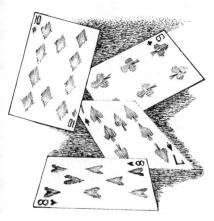

36 *heart*: life.
39 *come you now*: now you are saying.
42 *pledge*: surety.
43 *this' . . . chance*: this is a bad
business going.
44 *ancient*: of long standing.
pleasant: merry, amusing.
47 *Such*: the same.
48 *farther . . . home*: away from home.
49 *Where . . . grows*: where there's not
much opportunity.
in a few: briefly.
50 *thus it stands*: it's like this.
52 *this maze*: this bewildering world.
53 *Happily*: with any luck.
to . . . thrive: get married and do well
financially; Petruchio defies the
proverb, 'It is hard to wive and thrive
both in a year'.
54 *Crowns*: money.
55 *abroad*: away from home.
56 *come . . . thee*: speak plainly.
57 *wish . . . wife*: recommend a sharp-
tongued, bad-tempered wife to you.

30 was it fit for a servant to use his master so, being
perhaps, for aught I see, two and thirty, a pip out?
Whom would to God I had well knock'd at first,
Then had not Grumio come by the worst.
    Petruchio
A senseless villain! Good Hortensio,
35 I bade the rascal knock upon your gate
And could not get him for my heart to do it.
    Grumio
Knock at the gate? O heavens! Spake you not these
words plain: 'Sirrah, knock me here, rap me here, knock
me well, and knock me soundly'? And come you now
40 with 'knocking at the gate'?
    Petruchio
Sirrah, be gone, or talk not, I advise you.
    Hortensio
Petruchio, patience. I am Grumio's pledge.
Why this' a heavy chance 'twixt him and you—
Your ancient, trusty, pleasant servant Grumio.
45 And tell me now, sweet friend, what happy gale
Blows you to Padua here from old Verona?
    Petruchio
Such wind as scatters young men through the world
To seek their fortunes farther than at home
Where small experience grows. But, in a few,
50 Signor Hortensio, thus it stands with me:
Antonio my father is deceas'd
And I have thrust myself into this maze,
Happily to wive and thrive as best I may.
Crowns in my purse I have, and goods at home,
55 And so am come abroad to see the world.
    Hortensio
Petruchio, shall I then come roundly to thee
And wish thee to a shrewd ill-favour'd wife?
Thou'dst thank me but a little for my counsel—
And yet I'll promise thee she shall be rich,
60 And very rich. But th'art too much my friend,
And I'll not wish thee to her.
    Petruchio
Signor Hortensio, 'twixt such friends as we
Few words suffice, and therefore, if thou know

65 *burden*: musical accompaniment, refrain.
66 *as . . . love*: Sir Florent (a knight in Gower's *Confessio Amantis*) had to marry an ugly old woman to save his life.
67 *Sybil*: an aged prophetess of classical mythology; Apollo granted her as many years of life as the number of grains of sand in her hand.
68 *Socrates' Xanthippe*: The Greek philosopher's wife was notoriously bad-tempered.
69 *moves me not*: doesn't worry me.
70 *Affection's edge*: my keen desire.
72 *wive it wealthily*: make a rich marriage.
76 *aglet-baby*: small carved figure used as decorative tag at the end of a lace.
trot: hag.

77 *as . . . horses*: Horses (like modern cars) were always 'going wrong'.
78 *so*: provided that.
79 *are . . . in*: have got so far in this matter.
80 *broach'd in jest*: started to suggest as a joke.
85 *intolerable curst*: unbearably bad-tempered.
86 *froward*: perverse.
beyond all measure: extreme.
87 *state*: financial situation.
91 *board her*: woo her, Petruchio's image is from naval warfare.
chide: grumble.

97–8 *I . . . well*: The social world of Italy seems to be very confined (see 2, 1, 69).
98 *deceased*: deceasèd.

One rich enough to be Petruchio's wife—
65 As wealth is burden of my wooing dance—
Be she as foul as was Florentius' love,
As old as Sibyl, and as curst and shrewd
As Socrates' Xanthippe or a worse,
She moves me not, or not removes at least
70 Affection's edge in me, were she as rough
As are the swelling Adriatic seas.
I come to wive it wealthily in Padua;
If wealthily, then happily in Padua.
  Grumio
Nay, look you sir, he tells you flatly what his mind is. Why,
75 give him gold enough and marry him to a puppet or an
aglet-baby or an old trot with ne'er a tooth in her head,
though she have as many diseases as two and fifty horses.
Why, nothing comes amiss, so money comes withal.
  Hortensio
Petruchio, since we are stepp'd thus far in,
80 I will continue that I broach'd in jest.
I can, Petruchio, help thee to a wife
With wealth enough, and young, and beauteous,
Brought up as best becomes a gentlewoman.
Her only fault—and that is faults enough—
85 Is that she is intolerable curst,
And shrewd and froward so beyond all measure
That, were my state far worser than it is,
I would not wed her for a mine of gold!
  Petruchio
Hortensio, peace. Thou know'st not gold's effect.
90 Tell me her father's name and 'tis enough,
For I will board her though she chide as loud
As thunder when the clouds in autumn crack.
  Hortensio
Her father is Baptista Minola,
An affable and courteous gentleman.
95 Her name is Katherina Minola,
Renown'd in Padua for her scolding tongue.
  Petruchio
I know her father, though I know not her,
And he knew my deceased father well.
I will not sleep, Hortensio, till I see her,

100 *thus bold*: so rude.
101 *give you over*: leave you.

103 *while . . . lasts*: when he is in this mood.
A': upon.
104 *and*: if.

107 *rail . . . rope-tricks*: scold her in his own rhetoric.
108 *stand*: oppose, argue with.
109 *throw . . . with it*: answer her in such a way that she will be speechless; Petruchio's figure of speech will disable ('dis-figure') Katherina's vocabulary.
110 *she . . . cat*: Grumio's image is unclear, suggesting two cats scratching each other's eyes out.
112 *Tarry*: wait a moment.
113 *keep*: a) keeping; b) stronghold (of a castle).
116 *other more*: others besides me.

119 *before rehears'd*: already explained.

121 *order . . . tane*: Baptista has made this rule.

123 *curst*: cursed; but the sense is not so strong as 'damned'—perhaps 'perverse', or 'wilful'.

126 *do me grace*: do me a favour.
127 *in sober robes*: wearing an academic gown.
129 *Well seen*: fully qualified.

131 *make love*: i.e. declare his love.

---

100 And therefore let me be thus bold with you
To give you over at this first encounter—
Unless you will accompany me thither?
     Grumio
I pray you, sir, let him go while the humour lasts. A' my word, and she knew him as well as I do, she would think
105 scolding would do little good upon him. She may perhaps call him half a score knaves or so—why, that's nothing. And he begin once, he'll rail in his rope-tricks. I'll tell you what, sir, and she stand him but a little, he will throw a figure in her face and so disfigure her with it that
110 she shall have no more eyes to see withal than a cat. You know him not, sir.
     Hortensio
Tarry, Petruchio, I must go with thee,
For in Baptista's keep my treasure is.
He hath the jewel of my life in hold,
115 His youngest daughter, beautiful Bianca,
And her withholds from me and other more—
Suitors to her and rivals in my love—
Supposing it a thing impossible,
For those defects I have before rehears'd,
120 That ever Katherina will be wooed.
Therefore this order hath Baptista tane,
That none shall have access unto Bianca
Till Katherine the curst have got a husband.
     Grumio
'Katherine the curst'!
125 A title for a maid of all titles the worst.
     Hortensio
Now shall my friend Petruchio do me grace
And offer me disguis'd in sober robes
To old Baptista as a schoolmaster
Well seen in music, to instruct Bianca,
130 That so I may by this device at least
Have leave and leisure to make love to her
And unsuspected court her by herself.

Enter Gremio, *and* Lucentio *disguised as* Cambio, *a schoolmaster*

133 *beguile*: deceive.
134 *lay . . . together*: make plots.

Grumio
Here's no knavery! See, to beguile the old folks, how the
young folks lay their heads together. Master, master,
135 look about you! Who goes there, ha?
Hortensio
Peace, Grumio. It is the rival of my love.
Petruchio, stand by a while.
Grumio
A proper stripling, and an amorous!

138 *a proper stripling*: a fine young man:
Grumio is ironic.

They stand aside

139 *note*: the list of books.
140 *fairly bound*: Elizabethan books were
often sold unbound, and the
purchasers would put handsome
covers on them.
141 *at any hand*: in any case.
142 *see . . . her*: make sure you don't
teach her anything else.
144 *liberality*: generosity (in paying the
tutor's wages).
145 *mend . . . largess*: add something as a
present to you.
paper: the booklist referred to in line
139.

Gremio
O, very well, I have perus'd the note.
140 Hark you, sir, I'll have them very fairly bound—
All books of love, see that at any hand—
And see you read no other lectures to her:
You understand me. Over and beside
Signor Baptista's liberality
145 I'll mend it with a largess. Take your paper too
And let me have them very well perfum'd,
For she is sweeter than perfume itself
To whom they go to. What will you read to her?
Lucentio
Whate'er I read to her I'll plead for you
150 As for my patron, stand you so assur'd
As firmly as yourself were still in place—
Yea and perhaps with more successful words
Than you, unless you were a scholar, sir.
Gremio
O this learning, what a thing it is!
Grumio
155 [*Aside*] O this woodcock, what an ass it is!
Petruchio
[*Aside*] Peace, sirrah.
Hortensio
[*Aside*] Grumio, mum.

Coming forward

146 *them*: i.e. the books.
148 *read to her*: study with her.
151 *as . . . place*: as though you were
present yourself.
155 *woodcock*: a bird (of the snipe family)
noted for its foolishness.
157 *mum*: keep quiet.

God save you, Signor Gremio.

159 *Trow you*: do you know.

162 *lighted well*: discovered.

164 *fit . . . turn*: just what she needs.

172 *bags*: money-bags.

173 *vent*: talk about.
174 *speak me fair*: deal honestly with me.
175 *indifferent*: equally.

177 *Upon . . . liking*: if we can come to some satisfactory (financial) agreement with him; Hortensio has just invented this.

180 *So . . . done*: Gremio could be quoting either one of two proverbs: 'No sooner said than done', *and*, 'More easily said than done'.
181 *have . . . faults*: In the folktale versions of this story, the shrew's suitor is always warned about these.

184 *say'st me so*: is that all you have to say.

Gremio
And you are well met, Signor Hortensio.
Trow you whither I am going? To Baptista Minola.
160 I promis'd to enquire carefully
About a schoolmaster for the fair Bianca,
And by good fortune I have lighted well
On this young man, for learning and behaviour
Fit for her turn, well read in poetry
165 And other books—good ones, I warrant ye.
    Hortensio
'Tis well. And I have met a gentleman
Hath promis'd me to help me to another,
A fine musician to instruct our mistress.
So shall I no whit be behind in duty
170 To fair Bianca, so belov'd of me.
    Gremio
Belov'd of me, and that my deeds shall prove.
    Grumio
[*Aside*] And that his bags shall prove.
    Hortensio
Gremio, 'tis now no time to vent our love.
Listen to me, and if you speak me fair,
175 I'll tell you news indifferent good for either.
Here is a gentleman whom by chance I met, [*Presents
    Petruchio*]
Upon agreement from us to his liking,
Will undertake to woo curst Katherine,
Yea, and to marry her, if her dowry please.
    Gremio
180 So said, so done, is well.
Hortensio, have you told him all her faults?
    Petruchio
I know she is an irksome, brawling scold.
If that be all, masters, I hear no harm.
    Gremio
No? Say'st me so, friend? What countryman?
    Petruchio
185 Born in Verona, old Antonio's son.
My father dead, my fortune lives for me,

187 *good . . . see*: to have a long and
      happy life.

188 *were*: would be.

189 *if . . . name*: if that's what you want,
      get on with it, in God's name.

192 *or . . . her*: Grumio may be referring to
      some proverb such as 'Wedding and
      hanging go by destiny'.

193 *in that intent*: for that purpose.

195–201 *Have . . . clang*: Petruchio
      invents a heroic career for himself (he
      told Hortensio in lines 48–56 that this
      is his first venture 'abroad').

197 *chafed*: chafèd; enraged.

198 *ordnance*: cannon.
      field: battlefield.

200 *pitched*: pitchèd.

201 *'larums*: trumpet calls to arms.
      clang: The technical name for the
      sound of a military trumpet.

204 *chestnut*: the explosion of a roasted
      chestnut.

205 *fear . . . bugs*: frighten children with
      bugbears (= goblins).

207 *happily*: fortunately.

208 *yours*: Gremio tries to avoid paying
      Petruchio.

210 *charge of wooing*: the cost of his
      courtship.
      whatsoe'er: whatever it is.

212 *would*: wish.

And I do hope good days and long to see.
   Gremio
O sir, such a life with such a wife were strange.
But if you have a stomach, to't a God's name!
190 You shall have me assisting you in all.
But will you woo this wildcat?
   Petruchio
                 Will I live?
   Grumio
Will he woo her? Ay, or I'll hang her.
   Petruchio
Why came I hither but to that intent?
Think you a little din can daunt mine ears?
195 Have I not in my time heard lions roar?
Have I not heard the sea, puff'd up with winds,
Rage like an angry boar chafed with sweat?
Have I not heard great ordnance in the field,
And heaven's artillery thunder in the skies?
200 Have I not in a pitched battle heard
Loud 'larums, neighing steeds, and trumpets' clang?
And do you tell me of a woman's tongue
That gives not half so great a blow to hear
As will a chestnut in a farmer's fire?
205 Tush, tush, fear boys with bugs!
   Grumio
               For he fears none.
   Gremio
Hortensio, hark.
This gentleman is happily arriv'd,
My mind presumes, for his own good and yours.
   Hortensio
I promis'd we would be contributors
210 And bear his charge of wooing, whatsoe'er.
   Gremio
And so we will—provided that he win her.
   Grumio
I would I were as sure of a good dinner.

Enter Tranio *disguised as* Lucentio *and* Biondello

214 *readiest*: quickest.

216 *He . . . mean*: Biondello plays his supporting role to help Tranio.

217 *Even he*: that's exactly the man I mean.

218 *her to—*: Gremio suspects another rival, come to woo Bianca; but Tranio is impatient. The rhymed couplets of the following lines speed up the cross-talk.

219 *What . . . do*: what business is it of yours.

220 *at any hand*: in any case.

227 *so . . . she*: Bianca is not available for Tranio to woo.

230 *choice*: chosen.

232 *Softly*: take it easy; Tranio, pretending to be Lucentio, tries to talk like a courtly gentleman.

Tranio
Gentlemen, God save you. If I may be bold,
Tell me, I beseech you, which is the readiest way
215 To the house of Signor Baptista Minola?
Biondello
He that has the two fair daughters—is't he you mean?
Tranio
Even he, Biondello.
Gremio
Hark you, sir, you mean not her to—
Tranio
Perhaps him and her, sir. What have you to do?
Petruchio
220 Not her that chides, sir, at any hand, I pray.
Tranio
I love no chiders, sir. Biondello, let's away.
Lucentio
[*Aside*] Well begun, Tranio.
Hortensio
                              Sir, a word ere you go.
Are you a suitor to the maid you talk of, yea or no?
Tranio
And if I be, sir, is it any offence?
Gremio
225 No, if without more words you will get you hence.
Tranio
Why, sir, I pray, are not the streets as free
For me as for you?
Gremio
                              But so is not she.
Tranio
For what reason, I beseech you?
Gremio
For this reason, if you'll know—
230 That she's the choice love of Signor Gremio.
Hortensio
That she's the chosen of Signor Hortensio.
Tranio
Softly, my masters! If you be gentlemen,
Do me this right—hear me with patience.

235 *all*: entirely.

238 *Fair . . . daughter*: Helen of Troy, said
     to be the most beautiful woman in the
     world, who was stolen away from her
     Greek husband by the Trojan Paris—
     and became the cause of the Trojan
     War.
241 *speed alone*: be the only one to
     succeed.

243 *give him head*: let him run on (as
     though he were an unchecked horse).
     a jade: a weak horse that will quickly
     tire.

250 *let her go by*: leave her alone.

251–2 *leave . . . twelve*: Gremio implies
      that the wooing of Katherina will be as
      great a task as the twelve near-
      impossible 'labours' imposed on
      Hercules (Alcides), the superman of
      classical mythology.
253 *understand . . . sooth*: let me put it
     plainly.
254 *hearken for*: are interested in.

260 *stead*: help.
261 *break the ice*: get started.

263 *whose hap*: the man whose luck.
264 *graceless*: ill-bred.
     ingrate: ungrateful.

Baptista is a noble gentleman
235 To whom my father is not all unknown,
And were his daughter fairer than she is,
She may more suitors have, and me for one.
Fair Leda's daughter had a thousand wooers;
Then well one more may fair Bianca have.
240 And so she shall: Lucentio shall make one,
Though Paris came in hope to speed alone.
      Gremio
What, this gentleman will out-talk us all!
      Lucentio
Sir, give him head. I know he'll prove a jade.
      Petruchio
Hortensio, to what end are all these words?
      Hortensio
245 Sir, let me be so bold as ask you,
Did you yet ever see Baptista's daughter?
      Tranio
No, sir, but hear I do that he hath two,
The one as famous for a scolding tongue
As is the other for beauteous modesty.
      Petruchio
250 Sir, sir, the first's for me; let her go by.
      Gremio
Yea, leave that labour to great Hercules,
And let it be more than Alcides' twelve.
      Petruchio
Sir, understand you this of me in sooth:
The youngest daughter, whom you hearken for,
255 Her father keeps from all access of suitors
And will not promise her to any man
Until the elder sister first be wed.
The younger then is free, and not before.
      Tranio
If it be so, sir, that you are the man
260 Must stead us all, and me amongst the rest,
And if you break the ice and do this feat—
Achieve the elder, set the younger free
For our access—whose hap shall be to have her
Will not so graceless be to be ingrate.

265 *conceive*: understand.

267 *gratify*: reward; Hortensio is still
concerned that Petruchio shall be
paid for his task.

269 *slack*: slow in paying.
270 *contrive*: get together.
271 *quaff carouses*: drink toasts.
272 *adversaries*: opponents.

275 *motion*: suggestion.
276 *I . . . ben venuto*: I'll make you
welcome, I'll pay for you.

Hortensio
265 Sir, you say well, and well you do conceive;
And since you do profess to be a suitor,
You must, as we do, gratify this gentleman
To whom we all rest generally beholding.
Tranio
Sir, I shall not be slack; in sign whereof,
270 Please ye we may contrive this afternoon
And quaff carouses to our mistress' health,
And do as adversaries do in law,
Strive mightily, but eat and drink as friends.
Grumio and **Biondello**
O excellent motion! Fellows, let's be gone.
Hortensio
275 The motion's good indeed, and be it so.
Petruchio, I shall be your *ben venuto*.   [*Exeunt*

'Minion, thou liest! Is't not Hortensio?' (*2*, 1, 13). Charlotte Randle as Bianca and Monica Dolan as Katherina, Royal Shakespeare Company, 1999.

ACT 2

Act 2 Scene 1
Petruchio persists in his determination to court Katherina, despite her hostility. Hortensio and Lucentio are presented as tutors for Bianca, and Baptista listens to proposals from Bianca's suitors: Gremio's offer is generous—but he is outbidden by Tranio's inventiveness.

3 *gaud's*: trinkets—presumably jewellery given by her suitors.
4 *Unbind*: if you will unfasten.
5 *raiment*: clothes.

7 *my elders*: Such a reference to her age seems calculated to enrage Katherina.

8 *charge thee*: order you; 'thee' is omitted in the First Folio text.

13 *Minion*: A term of abuse for the spoilt favourite child.

14 *affect*: fancy, care for.

15 *but . . . him*: if there is no other way for you to have him.

16 *belike*: perhaps.

17 *fair*: fine, well-dressed.

18 *envy*: hate (the stress is on the second syllable).

SCENE 1

Padua: Baptista's house. Enter Katherina *and* Bianca *with her hands tied*

Bianca
Good sister, wrong me not, nor wrong yourself
To make a bondmaid and a slave of me.
That I disdain. But for these other gauds—
Unbind my hands, I'll pull them off myself,
5 Yea, all my raiment, to my petticoat,
Or what you will command me will I do,
So well I know my duty to my elders.
   Katherina
Of all thy suitors here I charge thee tell
Whom thou lov'st best. See thou dissemble not.
   Bianca
10 Believe me, sister, of all the men alive
I never yet beheld that special face
Which I could fancy more than any other.
   Katherina
Minion, thou liest! Is't not Hortensio?
   Bianca
If you affect him, sister, here I swear
15 I'll plead for you myself but you shall have him.
   Katherina
O then, belike, you fancy riches more:
You will have Gremio to keep you fair.
   Bianca
Is it for him you do envy me so?
Nay then, you jest, and now I well perceive
20 You have but jested with me all this while.
I prithee, sister Kate, untie my hands.

Katherina strikes her

Katherina
If that be jest, then all the rest was so.

Enter Baptista

Baptista
Why, how now, dame! Whence grows this insolence?
Bianca, stand aside. Poor girl, she weeps.

He unties her hands

23 *dame*: madam; a term of rebuke.
Baptista's partiality for his younger
daughter is evident, and may explain
some of Katherina's bitterness.

25 Go, ply thy needle; meddle not with her.
For shame, thou hilding of a devilish spirit!
Why dost thou wrong her that did ne'er wrong thee?
When did she cross thee with a bitter word?
    Katherina
Her silence flouts me, and I'll be reveng'd.

25 *ply thy needle*: get on with your
sewing.
meddle not: don't have anything to
do.
26 *hilding*: baggage.
28 *cross*: annoy.

29 *flouts*: mocks.

Flies after Bianca

Baptista
30 What, in my sight? Bianca, get thee in.　　　[*Exit* Bianca
    Katherina
What, will you not suffer me? Nay, now I see
She is your treasure, she must have a husband.
I must dance barefoot on her wedding day
And, for your love to her, lead apes in hell.
35 Talk not to me! I will go sit and weep
Till I can find occasion of revenge.　　　　　[*Exit*
    Baptista
Was ever gentleman thus griev'd as I?
But who comes here?

31 *suffer me*: leave me alone.

33 *dance . . . day*: behaviour traditionally
expected of an older, unmarried sister.
34 *for*: because of.
lead apes in hell: the proverbial fate
of an unmarried woman, who could
not lead children into heaven.

38s.d. *in the habit of a mean man*:
dressed like an ordinary man (i.e. not
like a gentleman).

Enter Gremio, Lucentio *in the habit of a mean man
disguised as* Cambio, Petruchio *with* Hortensio
disguised as Litio, Tranio *disguised as* Lucentio, *with
his boy* Biondello *bearing a lute and books*

Gremio
Good morrow, neighbour Baptista.

Baptista

40 Good morrow, neighbour Gremio. God save you,
     gentlemen.

Petruchio

And you, good sir. Pray have you not a daughter
Call'd Katherina, fair and virtuous?

Baptista

I have a daughter, sir, call'd Katherina.

Gremio

44 *orderly*: in the proper manner.

You are too blunt: go to it orderly.

Petruchio

45 You wrong me, Signor Gremio. Give me leave.
[*To* Baptista] I am a gentleman of Verona, sir,
That hearing of her beauty and her wit,
Her affability and bashful modesty,
Her wondrous qualities and mild behaviour,

50 *forward*: eager.

50 Am bold to show myself a forward guest
Within your house, to make mine eye the witness
Of that report which I so oft have heard.

53 *for an entrance*: as an entrance-fee.
entertainment: hospitable reception.

And for an entrance to my entertainment,
I do present you with a man of mine, [*Presents
     Hortensio*]

55 *Cunning*: expert.

55 Cunning in music and the mathematics,

56 *sciences*: subjects.

To instruct her fully in those sciences,
Whereof I know she is not ignorant.
Accept of him, or else you do me wrong.
His name is Litio, born in Mantua.

Baptista

60 *he*: he is welcome.

60 Y'are welcome, sir, and he for your good sake,
But for my daughter Katherine, this I know:

62 *for your turn*: the girl you want.

She is not for your turn, the more my grief.

Petruchio

I see you do not mean to part with her,
Or else you like not of my company.

Baptista

65 Mistake me not; I speak but as I find.

66 *What . . . name*: Baptista questions
with old-fashioned courtesy.

Whence are you, sir? What may I call your name?

Petruchio

Petruchio is my name, Antonio's son,
A man well known throughout all Italy.

69 *I . . . well*: Another example of the small world of Italian society (see *1, 2, 98*).
70 *Saving your tale*: with all respect to you.
71 *poor petitioners*: humble suitors.
72 *Backare*: stand back.

73 *I . . . doing*: I want to get on with it.

75 *grateful*: welcome.
76 *like*: same.
77 *kindly*: deeply; Gremio implies that Baptista has favoured his suit to Bianca.
79 *Rheims*: a famous university in northern France.
cunning in: knowledgeable about.
80 *the other*: i.e. Hortensio.
81 *Cambio*: The name that Lucentio has adopted means 'exchange' in Italian.

91 *resolve*: resolution.
92 *preferment*: the insistence that Katherina must be married before Bianca.
94 *upon . . . parentage*: when you know about my family.
98 *instrument*: i.e. the lute that Biondello is carrying.

Baptista
I know him well. You are welcome for his sake.
   Gremio
70 Saving your tale, Petruchio, I pray
Let us that are poor petitioners speak too.
Backare! You are marvellous forward.
   Petruchio
O pardon me, Signor Gremio, I would fain be doing.
   Gremio
I doubt it not, sir, but you will curse your wooing.
75 [*To* Baptista] Neighbour, this is a gift very grateful, I am
sure of it. To express the like kindness, myself, that have
been more kindly beholding to you than any, freely give
unto you this young scholar [*Presents* Lucentio] that
hath been long studying at Rheims, as cunning in
80 Greek, Latin and other languages as the other in music
and mathematics. His name is Cambio. Pray accept his
service.
   Baptista
A thousand thanks, Signor Gremio. Welcome, good
Cambio. [*To* Tranio] But, gentle sir, methinks you walk
85 like a stranger. May I be so bold to know the cause of
your coming?
   Tranio
Pardon me, sir, the boldness is mine own
That, being a stranger in this city here,
Do make myself a suitor to your daughter,
90 Unto Bianca, fair and virtuous.
Nor is your firm resolve unknown to me
In the preferment of the eldest sister.
This liberty is all that I request
That, upon knowledge of my parentage,
95 I may have welcome 'mongst the rest that woo,
And free access and favour as the rest,
And toward the education of your daughters
I here bestow a simple instrument
And this small packet of Greek and Latin books.

Biondello steps forward with the lute and books

101 *Lucentio . . . name*: Baptista perhaps
sees the name in one of the books.

103–4 *By . . . well*: I have heard good
reports of him.

106 *presently*: immediately.

111 *passing*: exceedingly.

113 *asketh*: demands.
114 *every . . . woo*: This line is found in
several old English ballads.
115 *in him me*: because of him you know
me.
116 *solely heir*: the only heir.
119 *dowry*: the father's financial
settlement on his daughter.
121 *in possession*: at the time of marriage;
this cash settlement may have been
unusually high because of Katherina's
temper.
122 *for*: in return for.
122–3 *assure . . . widowhood*: guarantee
her widow's rights; a widow did not
inherit her husband's estate (which
passed to his male heirs), but was
entitled to an allowance from it.
124 *lands . . . whatsoever*: his estate;
Petruchio uses the correct legal
terminology.
125 *specialties*: precise contracts.
126 *covenants*: financial undertakings.
on either hand: by both parties.

100 If you accept them, then their worth is great.
> **Baptista**

Lucentio is your name. Of whence, I pray?
> **Tranio**

Of Pisa, sir, son to Vincentio.
> **Baptista**

A mighty man of Pisa. By report
I know him well. You are very welcome, sir.
105 [*To* Hortensio] Take you the lute, [*To* Lucentio] and
> you the set of books;

You shall go see your pupils presently.
Holla, within!

Enter a Servant

> Sirrah, lead these gentlemen
To my daughters, and tell them both
These are their tutors. Bid them use them well.
> [*Exeunt* Servant, Hortensio, Lucentio
110 We will go walk a little in the orchard
And then to dinner. You are passing welcome,
And so I pray you all to think yourselves.
> **Petruchio**

Signor Baptista, my business asketh haste,
And every day I cannot come to woo.
115 You knew my father well, and in him me,
Left solely heir to all his lands and goods,
Which I have better'd rather than decreas'd.
Then tell me, if I get your daughter's love,
What dowry shall I have with her to wife?
> **Baptista**

120 After my death, the one half of my lands,
And in possession twenty thousand crowns.
> **Petruchio**

And for that dowry I'll assure her of
Her widowhood, be it that she survive me,
In all my lands and leases whatsoever.
125 Let specialties be therefore drawn between us,
That covenants may be kept on either hand.

Baptista
Ay, when the special thing is well obtain'd,
That is, her love, for that is all in all.
   Petruchio
Why, that is nothing, for I tell you, father,
130 I am as peremptory as she proud-minded,
And where two raging fires meet together
They do consume the thing that feeds their fury.
Though little fire grows great with little wind,
Yet extreme gusts will blow out fire and all.
135 So I to her, and so she yields to me,
For I am rough and woo not like a babe.
   Baptista
Well mayst thou woo, and happy be thy speed!
But be thou arm'd for some unhappy words.
   Petruchio
Ay, to the proof, as mountains are for winds,
140 That shakes not though they blow perpetually.

Enter Hortensio *with his head broke*

   Baptista
How now, my friend! Why dost thou look so pale?
   Hortensio
For fear, I promise you, if I look pale.
   Baptista
What, will my daughter prove a good musician?
   Hortensio
I think she'll sooner prove a soldier!
145 Iron may hold with her, but never lutes.
   Baptista
Why then, thou canst not break her to the lute?
   Hortensio
Why no, for she hath broke the lute to me.
I did but tell her she mistook her frets
And bow'd her hand to teach her fingering,
150 When, with a most impatient devilish spirit,
'Frets, call you these?' quoth she, 'I'll fume with them!'
And with that word she struck me on the head,
And through the instrument my pate made way,

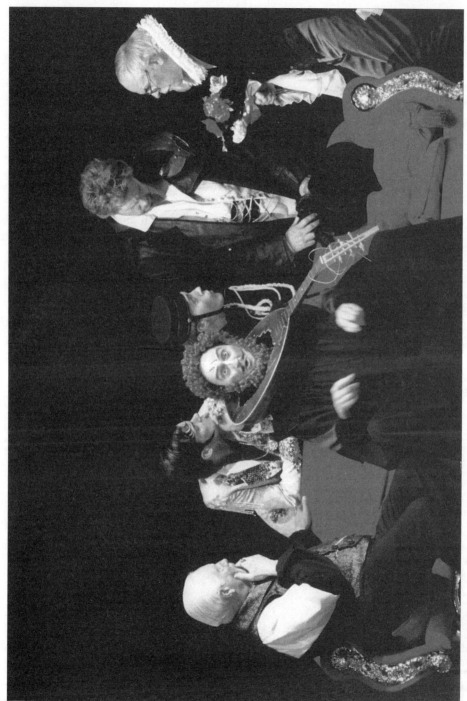

'I did but tell her she mistook her frets' (2, 1, 148). Clifford Rose as Baptista, Mark Lockyer as Tranio, Timothy Davies as Hortensio, Michael Siberry as Petruchio, and James Hayes as Gremio, Royal Shakespeare Company, 1995.

154 *amazed*: amazèd.

155 *pillary*: device for imprisoning a wrong-doer by restraining head and arms.

158 *As had she*: as though she had.
misuse: abuse.

159 *lusty*: spirited.

163 *Proceed in practice*: continue your teaching.
164 *apt*: ready.

167 *attend*: wait for.

168–80 *And . . . speak*: Petruchio's intimacy with the audience encourages them to appreciate the 'performance' he will give.
169 *rail*: shout at me.

175 *piercing*: moving.
176 *pack*: go away, clear off.

178 *deny*: refuse.
crave the day: ask her to name the day.
179 *ask the banns*: make a public declaration of an intent to marry (usually on three successive Sundays before the wedding).

182 *heard . . . hard*: Both words were pronounced 'hard', allowing Kate to make the first pun in an exchange of witty insults.

And there I stood amazed for a while,
155 As on a pillory, looking through the lute,
While she did call me rascal fiddler
And twangling Jack, with twenty such vile terms,
As had she studied to misuse me so.
        Petruchio
Now, by the world, it is a lusty wench!
160 I love her ten times more than e'er I did.
O how I long to have some chat with her.
        Baptista
[*To* Hortensio] Well, go with me, and be not so discomfited.
Proceed in practice with my younger daughter;
She's apt to learn and thankful for good turns.
165 Signor Petruchio, will you go with us,
Or shall I send my daughter Kate to you?
        Petruchio
I pray you do. I'll attend her here—
                    [*Exeunt all but* Petruchio
And woo her with some spirit when she comes!
Say that she rail, why then I'll tell her plain
170 She sings as sweetly as a nightingale.
Say that she frown, I'll say she looks as clear
As morning roses newly wash'd with dew.
Say she be mute and will not speak a word,
Then I'll commend her volubility
175 And say she uttereth piercing eloquence.
If she do bid me pack, I'll give her thanks
As though she bid me stay by her a week.
If she deny to wed, I'll crave the day
When I shall ask the banns, and when be married.

        Enter Katherina

180 But here she comes, and now, Petruchio, speak.
Good morrow, Kate, for that's your name, I hear.
        Katherina
Well have you heard, but something hard of hearing—
They call me Katherine that do talk of me.

186 *Christendom*: the entire Christian
    world.
187 *Kate-Hall*: This may have been some
    kind of topical joke, whose sense is
    now lost.
188 *dainties are all Kates*: delicacies are
    all called 'cates'.
189 *consolation*: comfort.
191 *sounded*: a) proclaimed; b) fathomed
    (as depth of water).
192 *to thee belongs*: as you deserve.

194 *in good time*: indeed.

196 *movable*: a piece of furniture that can
    be moved.

197 *A joint stool*: stool made by a joiner
    (a common insult).
    hit it: got it right.

198 *bear*: a) carry loads; b) bear children;
    c) carry the weight of a lover.

200 *jade*: worthless horse; Katherina
    implies that Petruchio lacks sexual
    stamina.

Petruchio
You lie, in faith, for you are call'd plain Kate,
185 And bonny Kate, and sometimes Kate the curst.
But Kate, the prettiest Kate in Christendom,
Kate of Kate-Hall, my super-dainty Kate—
For dainties are all Kates—and therefore, Kate,
Take this of me, Kate of my consolation:
190 Hearing thy mildness prais'd in every town,
Thy virtues spoke of and thy beauty sounded—
Yet not so deeply as to thee belongs—
Myself am mov'd to woo thee for my wife.
    Katherina
'Mov'd'—in good time! Let him that mov'd you hither
195 Remove you hence. I knew you at the first
You were a movable.
    Petruchio
             Why, what's a movable?
    Katherina
A joint stool.
    Petruchio
            Thou hast hit it. Come sit on me.
    Katherina
Asses are made to bear, and so are you.
    Petruchio
Women are made to bear, and so are you.
    Katherina
200 No such jade as you, if me you mean.

201 *burden*: a) lie heavy; b) accuse.

202 *light*: a) slender; b) promiscuous.

203 *swain*: country fellow.

204 *as heavy . . . be*: Katherina insists that she is completely honest (unlike clipped or counterfeit coins, whose weight betrays them).

205 *'Should . . . buzz*: Petruchio makes a feeble pun on the buzzing of a bee and 'buzz' = gossip.
tane: taken, caught in flight.
buzzard: a) a kind of hawk that cannot be trained; b) buzzing insect.

206 *turtle*: turtle-dove, symbol of faithful love.

207 *for . . . buzzard*: Katherina perhaps means that an untrained hawk can catch a dove just as a dove catches an insect.

214 *tales*: gossip—with a pun on 'tails' (= genital organs).

215 *come again*: have another try; Petruchio is preparing to start a fresh battle of words.

216 *try*: put to the test.

Petruchio
Alas, good Kate, I will not burden thee,
For, knowing thee to be but young and light—
  Katherina
Too light for such a swain as you to catch,
And yet as heavy as my weight should be.
  Petruchio
205 'Should be'! Should—buzz!
  Katherina
                Well tane, and like a buzzard.
  Petruchio
O slow-wing'd turtle, shall a buzzard take thee?
  Katherina
Ay, for a turtle, as he takes a buzzard.
  Petruchio
Come, come, you wasp! I'faith you are too angry.
  Katherina
If I be waspish, best beware my sting.
  Petruchio
210 My remedy is then to pluck it out.
  Katherina
Ay, if the fool could find it where it lies.
  Petruchio
Who knows not where a wasp does wear his sting?
In his tail.
  Katherina
      In his tongue.
  Petruchio
                Whose tongue?
  Katherina
Yours, if you talk of tales, and so farewell.

She turns to go

  Petruchio
215 What, with my tongue in your tail? Nay, come again.
Good Kate, I am a gentleman—
  Katherina
                That I'll try.

She strikes him

217 *cuff*: hit.
218 *So*: in that way.
     arms: coat of arms, which indicated
     the status of a gentleman.

221 *put . . . books*: a) register me as a
     gentleman; b) accept me in your
     favour.
222 *crest*: a) heraldic device; b) feathers
     on a bird's head.
     coxcomb: fool's cap (resembling the
     crest of a cock).

223 *combless*: harmless, non-aggressive.
224 *craven*: defeated fighting-cock.

226 *crab*: crab-apple (which is very sour).
229 *glass*: looking-glass.
230 *Well . . . one*: good guess for a
     beginner.
231 *too young*: too strong.

Petruchio
I swear I'll cuff you if you strike again.

He holds her

Katherina
So may you lose your arms.
If you strike me, you are no gentleman,
220 And if no gentleman, why then no arms.
  Petruchio
A herald, Kate? O put me in thy books.
  Katherina
What is your crest—a coxcomb?
  Petruchio
A combless cock, so Kate will be my hen.
  Katherina
No cock of mine; you crow too like a craven.
  Petruchio
225 Nay, come, Kate, come; you must not look so sour.
  Katherina
It is my fashion when I see a crab.
  Petruchio
Why, here's no crab, and therefore look not sour.
  Katherina
There is, there is.
  Petruchio
Then show it me.
  Katherina
                    Had I a glass I would.
  Petruchio
230 What, you mean my face?
  Katherina
                        Well aim'd of such a young one.
  Petruchio
Now, by Saint George, I am too young for you.
  Katherina
Yet you are wither'd.
  Petruchio
                    'Tis with cares.
  Katherina
                                I care not.

Petruchio
Nay, hear you, Kate—in sooth you scape not so.
Katherina
I chafe you if I tarry. Let me go.
Petruchio
235 Nay, not a whit. I find you passing gentle.
'Twas told me you were rough and coy and sullen,
And now I find report a very liar,
For thou art pleasant, gamesome, passing courteous,
But slow in speech, yet sweet as springtime flowers.
240 Thou canst not frown, thou canst not look askance,
Nor bite the lip as angry wenches will,
Nor hast thou pleasure to be cross in talk,
But thou with mildness entertain'st thy wooers,
With gentle conference, soft and affable.

He lets her go

245 Why does the world report that Kate doth limp?
O sland'rous world! Kate like the hazel twig
Is straight and slender, and as brown in hue
As hazel-nuts and sweeter than the kernels.
O let me see thee walk. Thou dost not halt.
Katherina
250 Go, fool, and whom thou keep'st command.
Petruchio
Did ever Dian so become a grove
As Kate this chamber with her princely gait?
O be thou Dian, and let her be Kate,
And then let Kate be chaste and Dian sportful!
Katherina
255 Where did you study all this goodly speech?
Petruchio
It is extempore, from my mother-wit.
Katherina
A witty mother! Witless else her son.
Petruchio
Am I not wise?
Katherina
                    Yes, keep you warm.

---

234 *I chafe you*: it will only excite you.

235 *not a whit*: not at all.
passing: exceedingly.
236 *coy*: disdainful.
237 *report . . . liar*: what they say is all
lies.
238 *gamesome*: full of fun.
courteous: ladylike.
240 *look askance*: glare.

242 *cross*: perverse.

244 *conference*: conversation.

249 *halt*: limp.

250 *whom . . . command*: A proverbial
saying—'give orders to your servants'.

251 *Dian*: Diana, Roman goddess of
hunting and chastity.
become: adorn.
252 *gait*: footsteps, walking.
254 *sportful*: playful, amorous.

256 *extempore*: made up on the spur of
the moment.
mother-wit: native intelligence.
257 *else*: otherwise.

258 *keep you warm*: with just enough
sense to keep you warm (a proverbial
saying).

259 *Marry*: by (the Virgin) Mary.
  mean: intend to.

261 *in plain terms*: to speak plainly.

262 *'greed*: agreed.

263 *will you, nill you*: whether you are
  willing or not (compare 'willy, nilly').

264 *for your turn*: just right for you.

269 *wild Kate*: Perhaps there is a pun with
  'wildcat'.

270 *Conformable*: tame, submissive.
  Kates: cates, sweet things (see
  line 188).

271 *Never make denial*: don't refuse me.

272 *to*: for.

273 *how speed you*: how are you getting
  on.

275 *speed amiss*: get on badly.

276 *in your dumps*: The modern form is
  'down in the dumps'—i.e. miserable.

280 *Jack*: knave, rascal.
281 *face*: brazen.
282 *all the world*: everybody.
283 *talk'd amiss of*: been wrong about.
284 *curst*: bad-tempered.
  for policy: deliberately, with some
  purpose.
285 *froward*: wilfully perverse.
286 *hot*: hot-tempered.
287 *Grissel*: the model of wifely patience
  and obedience whose story is told in
  Chaucer's *Canterbury Tales* ('The
  Clerk's Tale').
288 *Lucrece*: the model of wifely chastity,
  whose rape by Tarquin and
  subsequent suicide were described in
  Shakespeare's narrative poem *The
  Rape of Lucrece*.

Petruchio
Marry, so I mean, sweet Katherine, in thy bed.
260 And therefore, setting all this chat aside,
Thus in plain terms: your father hath consented
That you shall be my wife, your dowry 'greed on,
And will you, nill you, I will marry you.
Now Kate, I am a husband for your turn,
265 For, by this light whereby I see thy beauty—
Thy beauty that doth make me like thee well—
Thou must be married to no man but me,
For I am he am born to tame you, Kate,
And bring you from a wild Kate to a Kate
270 Conformable as other household Kates.

Enter Baptista, Gremio, *and* Tranio

Here comes your father. Never make denial—
I must and will have Katherine to my wife.
  Baptista
Now, Signor Petruchio, how speed you with my
  daughter?
  Petruchio
How but well, sir? How but well?
275 It were impossible I should speed amiss.
  Baptista
Why, how now, daughter Katherine, in your dumps?
  Katherina
Call you me 'daughter'? Now I promise you
You have show'd a tender fatherly regard
To wish me wed to one half lunatic,
280 A mad-cap ruffian and a swearing Jack
That thinks with oaths to face the matter out.
  Petruchio
Father, 'tis thus: yourself and all the world
That talk'd of her have talk'd amiss of her.
If she be curst, it is for policy,
285 For she's not froward, but modest as the dove;
She is not hot, but temperate as the morn;
For patience she will prove a second Grissel,
And Roman Lucrece for her chastity.

'. . . we have 'greed so well together That upon Sunday is the wedding day.' (2, 1, 289–90). Mark Lockyer as Tranio, James Hayes as Gremio, Michael Siberry as Petruchio, Clifford Rose as Baptista, and Josie Lawrence as Katherina, Royal Shakespeare Company, 1995.

And, to conclude, we have 'greed so well together
290 That upon Sunday is the wedding day.
    Katherina
I'll see thee hang'd on Sunday first!
    Gremio
Hark, Petruchio, she says she'll see thee hang'd first.
    Tranio
Is this your speeding? Nay then, goodnight our part.
    Petruchio
Be patient, gentlemen. I choose her for myself.
295 If she and I be pleas'd, what's that to you?
'Tis bargain'd 'twixt us twain, being alone,
That she shall still be curst in company.
I tell you, 'tis incredible to believe
How much she loves me—O the kindest Kate!
300 She hung about my neck, and kiss on kiss
She vied so fast, protesting oath on oath,
That in a twink she won me to her love.
O you are novices! 'Tis a world to see
How tame, when men and women are alone,
305 A meacock wretch can make the curstest shrew.
Give me thy hand, Kate. I will unto Venice,
To buy apparel 'gainst the wedding day.
Provide the feast, father, and bid the guests.
I will be sure my Katherine shall be fine.
    Baptista
310 I know not what to say, but give me your hands.
God send you joy, Petruchio! 'tis a match.
    Gremio and **Tranio**
Amen say we. We will be witnesses.
    Petruchio
Father, and wife, and gentlemen, adieu.
I will to Venice—Sunday comes apace.
315 We will have rings, and things, and fine array,
And kiss me, Kate, 'We will be married a' Sunday.'
             [*Exeunt* Petruchio *and* Katherina *separately*
    Gremio
Was ever match clapp'd up so suddenly?
    Baptista
Faith, gentlemen, now I play a merchant's part,
And venture madly on a desperate mart.

---

293 *speeding*: success.
goodnight our part: we can say goodbye to our share in the business (i.e. both to their promises to pay Petruchio's expenses and to their hopes of gaining Bianca).
296 *'twixt us twain*: between the two of us.
being alone: when we were alone.
297 *still*: always.

301 *vied*: redoubled: in gambling this is a term used for raising the stakes.
protesting: swearing.
302 *in a twink*: in the twinkling of an eye.
303 *'Tis a world*: it is worth a world.

305 *meacock*: feeble.
306 *will*: will go.
307 *'gainst*: ready for.
308 *bid*: invite.

310–11 *give . . . match*: Joining hands before witnesses formed a 'pre-contract', which was more binding than a modern engagement.

314 *apace*: quickly.

316 *'We . . . Sunday'*: The refrain of several popular ballads.

317 *clapp'd up*: fixed up; market bargains were struck by clapping hands.

319 *venture . . . mart*: speculate wildly in a risky market.

320 *commodity*: piece of merchandise.
     lay fretting by you: was going to waste;
     and was irritating you.

325 *looked for*: lookèd; been waiting for.
329 *Youngling*: youngster, young man.
     dear: a) affectionately; b) at such
     expense.
330 *doth fry*: is too hot.
331 *Skipper*: playboy, laddie.
333 *compound*: settle.
334 *deeds*: actions; financial
     arrangements.
     he of both: whichever of you two;
     Hortensio has been forgotten.
335 *dower*: widow's allowance (see above,
     122–3 note).
339 *furnished*: furnishèd.
     plate: domestic utensils of silver and
     gold.
340 *lave*: wash.
341 *hangings*: wall-coverings.
     Tyrian: purple (the dye was originally
     made at Tyre).

342 *coffers*: money-chests.
343 *cypress*: wood prized for fragrance.
     arras counterpoints: counterpanes
     made of Arras tapestry.
344 *tents, and canopies*: bed-curtains and
     hangings.
345 *boss'd*: embossed, embroidered.
346 *Valance . . . needlework*: fringe of bed
     canopy embroidered with gold thread
     from Venice.
349 *milch-kine . . . pail*: cows whose milk
     is sold for human consumption.

Tranio
320 'Twas a commodity lay fretting by you.
    'Twill bring you gain, or perish on the seas.
Baptista
    The gain I seek is quiet in the match.
Gremio
    No doubt but he hath got a quiet catch!
    But now, Baptista, to your younger daughter:
325 Now is the day we long have looked for;
    I am your neighbour and was suitor first.
Tranio
    And I am one that love Bianca more
    Than words can witness, or your thoughts can guess.
Gremio
    Youngling, thou canst not love so dear as I.
Tranio
330 Greybeard, thy love doth freeze.
Gremio
                                But thine doth fry.
    Skipper, stand back! 'Tis age that nourisheth.
Tranio
    But youth in ladies' eyes that flourisheth.
Baptista
    Content you, gentlemen; I will compound this strife.
    'Tis deeds must win the prize, and he of both
335 That can assure my daughter greatest dower
    Shall have my Bianca's love.
    Say, Signor Gremio, what can you assure her?
Gremio
    First, as you know, my house within the city
    Is richly furnished with plate and gold,
340 Basins and ewers to lave her dainty hands;
    My hangings all of Tyrian tapestry;
    In ivory coffers I have stuff'd my crowns,
    In cypress chests my arras counterpoints,
    Costly apparel, tents, and canopies,
345 Fine linen, Turkey cushions boss'd with pearl,
    Valance of Venice gold in needlework,
    Pewter and brass, and all things that belongs
    To house or housekeeping. Then at my farm
    I have a hundred milch-kine to the pail,

350 *oxen*: beef cattle.

351 *answerable . . . portion*: in proportion to this estate.

352 *struck in years*: handicapped by age.

355 *came well in*: was well said.
list: listen.

356 *I am . . . heir*: Tranio, pretending to be Lucentio, will increase the bidding— from his own imagination.

361–2 *two thousand . . . land*: a substantial annual income ('ducats' = Venetian gold coins) from arable land.

362 *jointure*: settlement to provide for widowhood (see 122–3 note).

366 *argosy*: largest class of merchant ship.

367 *Marsellis' road*: the safe anchorage outside the harbour of Marseilles; the Folio spelling indicates pronunciation.

368 *chok'd*: beaten your offer.

370 *galliasses*: ships, larger than galleys, using both sails and oars.

371 *tight*: sound, watertight.

377 *out-vied*: outbidden; see line 301.

380 *else*: otherwise.

382 *cavil*: legal trifle.

---

350 Six score fat oxen standing in my stalls,
And all things answerable to this portion.
Myself am struck in years I must confess,
And if I die tomorrow this is hers,
If whilst I live she will be only mine.

Tranio

355 That 'only' came well in. Sir, list to me:
I am my father's heir and only son.
If I may have your daughter to my wife,
I'll leave her houses three or four as good
Within rich Pisa walls as any one
360 Old Signor Gremio has in Padua,
Besides two thousand ducats by the year
Of fruitful land, all which shall be her jointure.
What, have I pinch'd you, Signor Gremio?

Gremio

Two thousand ducats by the year of land?
365 [*Aside*] My land amounts not to so much in all!—
That she shall have, besides an argosy
That now is lying in Marsellis' road.—
What, have I chok'd you with an argosy?

Tranio

Gremio, 'tis known my father hath no less
370 Than three great argosies, besides two galliasses
And twelve tight galleys. These I will assure her,
And twice as much whate'er thou off'rest next.

Gremio

Nay, I have offer'd all. I have no more,
And she can have no more than all I have.
375 If you like me, she shall have me and mine.

Tranio

Why, then the maid is mine from all the world
By your firm promise. Gremio is out-vied.

Baptista

I must confess your offer is the best,
And, let your father make her the assurance,
380 She is your own; else, you must pardon me.
If you should die before him, where's her dower?

Tranio

That's but a cavil. He is old, I young.

Gremio

And may not young men die as well as old?

Baptista

Well, gentlemen, I am thus resolv'd.
385 On Sunday next you know
My daughter Katherine is to be married.
Now, on the Sunday following shall Bianca
Be bride to you, if you make this assurance.
If not, to Signor Gremio.
390 And so I take my leave, and thank you both.

Gremio

Adieu, good neighbour.   [*Exit* Baptista
                    Now I fear thee not.
Sirrah, young gamester, your father were a fool
To give thee all and in his waning age
Set foot under thy table. Tut, a toy!
395 An old Italian fox is not so kind, my boy.   [*Exit*

Tranio

A vengeance on your crafty wither'd hide!
Yet I have fac'd it with a card of ten.
'Tis in my head to do my master good:
I see no reason but suppos'd Lucentio
400 Must get a father called suppos'd Vincentio.
And that's a wonder—fathers commonly
Do get their children, but in this case of wooing
A child shall get a sire, if I fail not of my cunning.
                                        [*Exit*

392 *gamester*: gambler.
    were: would be.
393 *waning age*: declining years.
394 *Set . . . table*: be dependent on you.
    toy: ridiculous idea.
395 *not so kind*: i.e. cannot be fooled so
    easily.
397 *fac'd . . . ten*: The expression, deriving
    from a card-game called Primero,
    seems to indicate that Tranio is
    winning at the moment—by bluffing.
399 *see no reason*: can't see any other
    way.
    suppos'd Lucentio: the man who is
    supposed to be Lucentio—i.e.
    himself.
400 *suppos'd Vincentio*: who is supposed
    to be Vincentio (Lucentio's father—
    see *1*, 1, 13).
402 *get*: beget.

ACT 3

Act 3 Scene 1
Lucentio and Hortensio compete for
Bianca's attention in their lessons.

Scene 1

Padua: Baptista's house. Enter Lucentio *as* Cambio,
Hortensio *as* Litio, *and* Bianca

Lucentio
Fiddler, forbear! You grow too forward, sir.
Have you so soon forgot the entertainment
Her sister Katherine welcom'd you withal?
    Hortensio
But, wrangling pedant, this is
5 The patroness of heavenly harmony.
Then give me leave to have prerogative,
And when in music we have spent an hour,
Your lecture shall have leisure for as much.
    Lucentio
Preposterous ass, that never read so far
10 To know the cause why music was ordain'd!
Was it not to refresh the mind of man
After his studies or his usual pain?
Then give me leave to read philosophy
And, while I pause, serve in your harmony.
    Hortensio
15 Sirrah! I will not bear these braves of thine!
    Bianca
Why, gentlemen, you do me double wrong
To strive for that which resteth in my choice.
I am no breeching scholar in the schools:
I'll not be tied to hours nor 'pointed times
20 But learn my lessons as I please myself.
And, to cut off all strife, here sit we down.
Take you your instrument; play you the whiles;
His lecture will be done ere you have tun'd.
    Hortensio
You'll leave his lecture when I am in tune?

1 *forward*: impertinent; perhaps
  Hortensio is now trying to guide
  Bianca's hand (compare *2*, 1, 149).
2 *entertainment*: reception.

4 *wrangling*: disputatious,
  argumentative.
5 *patroness*: Hortensio flatters Bianca:
  St Cecilia is the patron saint of music.
6 *prerogative*: precedence; music was
  held to be the highest form of study.
8 *lecture*: lesson.
  leisure . . .much: just as much time.
9 *Preposterous*: ridiculous (literally,
  'getting things back to front'; Lucentio
  speaks like a pedantic schoolmaster).
  read: learned.
12 *usual pain*: regular labours.

13 *read*: teach.

14 *serve in*: serve up (like part of a meal).

15 *braves*: insults.

16 *do . . . wrong*: both wrong me.

17 *resteth . . . choice*: is for me to
   decide.
18 *breeching*: a) wearing breeches;
   b) liable to be whipped.

22 *the whiles*: for a time.

24 *in tune*: a) tuned up; b) in favour.

Lucentio

25 That will be never. Tune your instrument.

Bianca

Where left we last?

Lucentio

Here, madam. [*He reads*]
Hic ibat Simois, hic est Sigeia tellus,
Hic steterat Priami regia celsa senis.

Bianca

30 Conster them.

Lucentio

Hic ibat—as I told you before; *Simois*—I am Lucentio;
hic est—son unto Vincentio of Pisa; *Sigeia tellus*—
disguised thus to get your love. *Hic steterat*—and that
Lucentio that comes a-wooing; *Priami*—is my man

35 Tranio; *regia*—bearing my port; *celsa senis*—that we
might beguile the old pantaloon.

Hortensio

Madam, my instrument's in tune.

Bianca

Let's hear. [*He plays*] O fie! The treble jars.

Lucentio

Spit in the hole, man, and tune again.

Bianca

40 Now let me see if I can conster it. *Hic ibat Simois*—I
know you not; *hic est Sigeia tellus*—I trust you not; *Hic*
steterat Priami—take heed he hear us not; *regia*—
presume not; *celsa senis*—despair not.

Hortensio

Madam, 'tis now in tune.

He plays again

Lucentio

                    All but the bass.

Hortensio

45 The bass is right; 'tis the base knave that jars.
[*Aside*] How fiery and forward our pedant is!
Now, for my life, the knave doth court my love.
Pedascule, I'll watch you better yet.

28–9 *'Hic . . . senis'*: 'Here ran the river Simois; here is the Sigeian land [Troy]; here stood old Priam's lofty palace' (Ovid, *Heroides* I, 33–4).

30 *Conster*: translate; Bianca uses an old form (stressed on the first syllable) of 'construe'.

31 *as . . . before*: Lucentio's mock translation gives him a chance to declare his love.

35 *bearing my port*: taking my place.

36 *beguile*: cheat.
pantaloon: i.e. Gremio; compare *1, 1, 45s.d.* Lucentio does not think of the disguised Hortensio as a rival.

38 *jars*: is discordant.

39 *Spit . . . hole*: try again—from the proverb 'Spit in your hands and take better hold'.

40–3 *Now . . . not*: Bianca's own translation gives warning to her impetuous suitor.

45 *bass*: bass string; but Hortensio's pun shows his suspicion.

48 *Pedascule*: little schoolmaster; a contemptuous coinage.
better yet: even better.

'Call you this "gamut"? Tut, I like it not!' (*3*, 1, 77). Dermot Kerrigan as Lucentio, Timothy Davies as Hortensio, and Tilly Blackwood as Bianca, Royal Shakespeare Company, 1995.

Bianca
In time I may believe, yet I mistrust.
    Lucentio
50 Mistrust it not, for sure Aeacides
Was Ajax, call'd so from his grandfather.
    Bianca
I must believe my master, else, I promise you,
I should be arguing still upon that doubt.
But let it rest. Now, Litio, to you.
55 Good master, take it not unkindly, pray,
That I have been thus pleasant with you both.
    Hortensio
[*To* Lucentio] You may go walk, and give me leave
    awhile.
My lessons make no music in three parts.
    Lucentio
Are you so formal, sir? Well, I must wait—
60 [*Aside*] And watch withal, for, but I be deceiv'd,
Our fine musician groweth amorous.
    Hortensio
Madam, before you touch the instrument
To learn the order of my fingering,
I must begin with rudiments of art,
65 To teach you gamut in a briefer sort,
More pleasant, pithy, and effectual
Than hath been taught by any of my trade;
And there it is in writing, fairly drawn.
    Bianca
Why, I am past my gamut long ago.
    Hortensio
70 Yet read the gamut of Hortensio.
    Bianca
[*Reads*] '*Gamut* I am, the ground of all accord:
A re, to plead Hortensio's passion;
B mi, Bianca, take him for thy lord;
C fa ut, that loves with all affection;
75 *D sol re*, one clef, two notes have I;
E la mi, show pity or I die.'
Call you this 'gamut'? Tut, I like it not!
Old fashions please me best. I am not so nice
To change true rules for odd inventions.

50–1 *Aeacides . . . Ajax*: Aeacides (= 'descendant of Aeacus') is another name of Ajax; Lucentio returns to Ovid.

56 *pleasant*: merry.

57 *give me leave*: leave me alone.

58 *three parts*: Song books often showed three harmonizing parts on the same page, so that singers could gather round the same book.

60 *withal*: as well.
    but: unless.

63 *order*: method.
64 *begin . . . art*: begin at the very beginning.
65 *gamut*: the musical scale.

68 *fairly drawn*: completely written out.

71–6 '*Gamut . . . die*': Hortensio has found a clever way of declaring his love with the notes of the musical scale (as in the film *The Sound of Music*).

78 *nice*: fussy.

Enter a Servant

Servant

80 Mistress, your father prays you leave your books,
And help to dress your sister's chamber up.
You know tomorrow is the wedding-day.
   Bianca
Farewell, sweet masters both, I must be gone.
                                    [*Exeunt* Bianca *and* Servant
   Lucentio
Faith, mistress, then I have no cause to stay.   [*Exit*
   Hortensio
85 But I have cause to pry into this pedant:
Methinks he looks as though he were in love.
Yet if thy thoughts, Bianca, be so humble
To cast thy wand'ring eyes on every stale,
Seize thee that list! If once I find thee ranging
90 Hortensio will be quit with thee by changing.   [*Exit*

88 *stale*: decoy-bird.
89 *Seize thee that list*: anyone can have you.
   ranging: straying.
90 *be quit*: get even.

Act 3 Scene 2
The wedding day. Petruchio, strangely dressed, arrives late, rushes Katherina to the church, then carries her off home with him.

SCENE 2

Padua: Baptista's *house. Enter* Baptista, Gremio, Tranio *disguised as* Lucentio, Katherina, Bianca, Lucentio *disguised as* Cambio, *other* Guests *and* Attendants

Baptista
[*To* Tranio] Signor Lucentio, this is the 'pointed day
That Katherine and Petruchio should be married,
And yet we hear not of our son-in-law.
What will be said? What mockery will it be
5 To want the bridegroom when the priest attends
To speak the ceremonial rites of marriage!
What says Lucentio to this shame of ours?
   Katherina
No shame but mine. I must, forsooth, be forc'd
To give my hand, oppos'd against my heart,
10 Unto a mad-brain rudesby, full of spleen,
Who woo'd in haste and means to wed at leisure.
I told you, I, he was a frantic fool,
Hiding his bitter jests in blunt behaviour.

5 *want*: lack.

8 *forsooth*: indeed.
9 *oppos'd . . . heart*: against my will.
10 *rudesby*: lout.
   full of spleen: intemperate: the spleen was thought to be the seat of both melancholic depression and excitability.
11 *woo'd . . . leisure*: Katherina adapts the proverb, 'marry in haste and repent at leisure'.

14 *to . . . for*: to get a reputation as.

15 *'point*: fix.

16 *banns*: announcements; see *2*, 1, 179 note.

21–5 *Patience . . . honest*: This intimacy would be more appropriate for Hortensio, Petruchio's 'best beloved and approved friend' (*1*, 2, 3), and suggests the play is not fully revised.

22 *means but well*: has only the best intentions.

23 *stays him from*: prevents from keeping.

24 *passing*: exceedingly.

25 *be merry*: jokes a lot.
   withal: at the same time.

26 *Would*: I wish.

28 *a very saint*: even a saint.

29 *humour*: temper.

30 *old*: strange; in the Folio text, Biondello says simply 'such news', but Baptista's response justifies the usual emendation.

And to be noted for a merry man,
15 He'll woo a thousand, 'point the day of marriage,
   Make feast, invite friends, and proclaim the banns,
   Yet never means to wed where he hath woo'd.
   Now must the world point at poor Katherine
   And say, 'Lo, there is mad Petruchio's wife
20 If it would please him come and marry her!'
      Tranio
   Patience, good Katherine, and Baptista too.
   Upon my life, Petruchio means but well,
   Whatever fortune stays him from his word.
   Though he be blunt, I know him passing wise;
25 Though he be merry, yet withal he's honest.
      Katherina
   Would Katherine had never seen him though!
                    [*Exit weeping followed by* Bianca *and others*
      Baptista
   Go, girl. I cannot blame thee now to weep,
   For such an injury would vex a very saint,
   Much more a shrew of thy impatient humour.

      Enter Biondello

      Biondello
30 Master, master, news! And such old news as you never
   heard of!
      Baptista
   Is it new and old too? How may that be?
      Biondello
   Why, is it not news to hear of Petruchio's coming?
      Baptista
   Is he come?
      Biondello
35 Why no, sir.
      Baptista
   What then?
      Biondello
   He is coming.
      Baptista
   When will he be here?

40 *what to*: what about.
42 *jerkin*: jacket.
   turned: turned inside out.
43 *candle-cases*: i.e. worn out and used
   for storing candles.
45 *chapeless*: without a sheath.
46 *points*: tagged laces fastening doublet
   and hose.
   hipped: with a dislocated hip.
   mothy: moth-eaten.
47 *of no kindred*: not matching.
   possessed with: afflicted with;
   Biondello's catalogue of equine
   diseases would have been as familiar
   to the original hearers as an account
   of the mechanical failings of an old
   car.
48 *glanders*: disease causing swelling of
   the jaw, with watery discharge from
   the nostrils.
   like . . . chine: liable to crumble in
   the spine.
48–9 *troubled . . . fashions*: suffering
   from other diseases affecting the
   mouth.
50 *windgalls*: tumours on the fetlocks.
   sped . . . spavins: ruined with swollen
   leg-joints.
   rayed . . . yellows: discoloured with
   jaundice.
51 *fives*: swellings behind the ears.
   stark: utterly.
   staggers: disease causing
   unsteadiness.
52 *begnawn . . . bots*: eaten by intestinal
   worms.
   swayed: sagging.
53 *shoulder-shotten*: with dislocated
   shoulder.
   near-legged before: knock-kneed in
   front.
53–4 *with . . . leather*: with a broken bit
   and a halter made of sheep skin (i.e.
   not cowhide).
55 *restrained*: drawn up tight.
56 *girth*: saddle-strap going under horse's
   belly.
57 *pieced*: patched, mended.
   crupper: strap passing under the
   horse's tail to hold the saddle steady.
   velour: velvet-like fabric.
58 *two . . . studs*: her initials set in
   studs.
59 *packthread*: string (for tying packets).
61 *lackey*: footman.
   for . . . world: in every respect.
   caparisoned: dressed up.

Biondello
When he stands where I am and sees you there.
Tranio
40 But say, what to thine old news?
Biondello
Why, Petruchio is coming in a new hat and an old
jerkin; a pair of old breeches thrice turned; a pair of
boots that have been candle-cases, one buckled, another
laced; an old rusty sword tane out of the town armoury,
45 with a broken hilt and chapeless; with two broken
points; his horse hipped—with an old mothy saddle
and stirrups of no kindred—besides, possessed with the
glanders and like to mose in the chine; troubled with
the lampass, infected with the fashions, full of
50 windgalls, sped with spavins, rayed with the yellows,
past cure of the fives, stark spoiled with the staggers,
begnawn with the bots, swayed in the back and
shoulder-shotten, near-legged before, and with a half-
cheeked bit and a headstall of sheep's leather, which,
55 being restrained to keep him from stumbling, hath been
often burst and now repaired with knots; one girth six
times pieced, and a woman's crupper of velour, which
hath two letters for her name fairly set down in studs,
and here and there pieced with packthread.
Baptista
60 Who comes with him?
Biondello
O sir, his lackey, for all the world caparisoned like the
horse, with a linen stock on one leg and a kersey boot-
hose on the other, gartered with a red and blue list; an
old hat and the humour of forty fancies pricked in't for
65 a feather; a monster, a very monster in apparel, and not
like a Christian footboy or a gentleman's lackey.
Tranio
'Tis some odd humour pricks him to this fashion,
Yet oftentimes he goes but mean-apparell'd.
Baptista
I am glad he's come, howsoe'er he comes.
Biondello
70 Why, sir, he comes not.
Baptista
Didst thou not say he comes?

62 *stock*: stocking.
62–3 *kersey boot-hose*: woollen
    overstocking.
63 *list*: strip of cloth.
64 *the humour . . . fancies*: some wildly
    fantastical arrangement; the exact
    sense is obscure.
    pricked in't: pinned on it.
67 *odd . . . pricks*: strange mood that
    incites.
68 *mean-apparell'd*: poorly dressed.
75 *all one*: the same thing.
76 *Saint Jamy*: St James; there is no
    known source of Biondello's rhyme.
77 *hold*: bet.

80 *many*: a company ('meiny').

81 *be*: are.
    gallants: lads.

82 *not well*: i.e. not well dressed.

83 *halt not*: are not lame.

87 *Gentles*: gentlemen.
    methinks: it seems to me that.
88 *goodly*: worthy.
89 *monument*: omen.
90 *comet*: Comets were thought to be
    warnings of disaster.
    prodigy: portent.

93 *unprovided*: unprepared.
94 *doff this habit*: take off these clothes.
    shame to your estate: a disgrace for a
    man in your position.
95 *solemn festival*: ceremonies.

Biondello
Who? That Petruchio came?
    Baptista
Ay, that Petruchio came.
    Biondello
No, sir, I say his horse comes with him on his back.
    Baptista
75 Why, that's all one.
    Biondello
        Nay, by Saint Jamy.
    I hold you a penny,
    A horse and a man
    Is more than one,
80   And yet not many.

Enter Petruchio *and* Grumio

    Petruchio
Come, where be these gallants? Who's at home?
    Baptista
You are welcome, sir.
    Petruchio
                And yet I come not well.
    Baptista
And yet you halt not.
    Tranio
                Not so well apparell'd
As I wish you were.
    Petruchio
85 Were it better, I should rush in thus.
But where is Kate? Where is my lovely bride?
How does my father? Gentles, methinks you frown,
And wherefore gaze this goodly company
As if they saw some wondrous monument,
90 Some comet or unusual prodigy?
    Baptista
Why, sir, you know this is your wedding-day.
First were we sad, fearing you would not come,
Now sadder that you come so unprovided.
Fie, doff this habit, shame to your estate,
95 An eye-sore to our solemn festival.

96 *occasion of import*: important matter.

97 *all so long*: for so very long.

98 *unlike yourself*: Tranio, who had explained that Petruchio 'oftentimes . . . goes but mean-apparelled' (line 68) now appears anxious to reassure Baptista.

100 *Sufficeth*: let it be enough.

101 *enforced*: enforcèd.
    digress: change my plans.

105 *wears*: is passing.

106 *unreverent*: disrespectful.

110 *Good sooth*: yes indeed.
    ha' done with: that's enough of.

112 *wear*: wear out—i.e. by sexually exhausting him.

113 *accoutrements*: attire.

117 *lovely*: loving.

118 *meaning in*: reason for.

121 *I'll after*: I'll go after.
    event: outcome.

122–3 *to love . . . liking*: it's important that we should get her father's approval as well as Bianca's love; the short conversation of Tranio and Lucentio must allow time for the happenings that Gremio will describe.

123 *bring to pass*: achieve.

124 *As . . . imparted*: as I told you earlier.

Tranio
And tell us what occasion of import
Hath all so long detain'd you from your wife
And sent you hither so unlike yourself.
    Petruchio
Tedious it were to tell, and harsh to hear.
100 Sufficeth I am come to keep my word
Though in some part enforced to digress,
Which at more leisure I will so excuse
As you shall well be satisfied with all.
But where is Kate? I stay too long from her.
105 The morning wears, 'tis time we were at church.
    Tranio
See not your bride in these unreverent robes;
Go to my chamber, put on clothes of mine.
    Petruchio
Not I, believe me; thus I'll visit her.
    Baptista
But thus, I trust, you will not marry her.
    Petruchio
110 Good sooth, even thus. Therefore ha' done with words;
To me she's married, not unto my clothes.
Could I repair what she will wear in me
As I can change these poor accoutrements,
'Twere well for Kate and better for myself.
115 But what a fool am I to chat with you
When I should bid good morrow to my bride
And seal the title with a lovely kiss!
                    [*Exit with* Grumio
    Tranio
He hath some meaning in his mad attire.
We will persuade him, be it possible,
120 To put on better ere he go to church.
    Baptista
I'll after him and see the event of this.
            [*Exit with* Gremio, Biondello, *and* Attendants.
    Tranio
[*To* Lucentio] But, sir, to love concerneth us to add
Her father's liking, which to bring to pass,
As I before imparted to your worship,
125 I am to get a man—whate'er he be

126 *skills not much*: doesn't matter much.
fit . . . turn: make him serve our
purpose.
128 *make assurance*: guarantee.
129 *promised*: promisèd.

134 *steal our marriage*: get married
secretly.
135 *say no*: forbid it.

137 *by degrees*: gradually.
138 *watch our vantage*: wait for an
opportunity.
139–42 *We'll . . . Lucentio*: These lines
appear to be addressed to the
audience.
139 *overreach*: out-do, beat.
140 *narrow-prying*: watchful, suspicious.
141 *quaint*: ingenious, crafty.

146 *groom*: rough fellow.

150 *the devil's dam*: the devil's mother—
who was worse than her son.

151 *fool*: harmless innocent.
to: compared to.
154 *by gogs-wouns*: by God's (Christ's)
wounds; a fairly common oath at this
time.

It skills not much, we'll fit him to our turn—
And he shall be Vincentio of Pisa
And make assurance here in Padua
Of greater sums than I have promised.
130 So shall you quietly enjoy your hope
And marry sweet Bianca with consent.
　　Lucentio
Were it not that my fellow schoolmaster
Doth watch Bianca's steps so narrowly,
'Twere good, methinks, to steal our marriage,
135 Which once perform'd, let all the world say no,
I'll keep mine own despite of all the world.
　　Tranio
That by degrees we mean to look into
And watch our vantage in this business.
We'll overreach the greybeard Gremio,
140 The narrow-prying father Minola,
The quaint musician, amorous Litio,
All for my master's sake, Lucentio.

　　Enter Gremio

Signor Gremio! Came you from the church?
　　Gremio
As willingly as e'er I came from school.
　　Tranio
145 And is the bride and bridegroom coming home?
　　Gremio
A bridegroom, say you? 'Tis a groom indeed—
A grumbling groom, and that the girl shall find.
　　Tranio
Curster than she? Why, 'tis impossible.
　　Gremio
Why, he's a devil, a devil, a very fiend!
　　Tranio
150 Why, she's a devil, a devil, the devil's dam!
　　Gremio
Tut, she's a lamb, a dove, a fool, to him.
I'll tell you, Sir Lucentio: when the priest
Should ask if Katherine should be his wife,
'Ay, by gogs-wouns!' quoth he, and swore so loud

155 That, all-amaz'd, the priest let fall the book,
And as he stoop'd again to take it up,
This mad-brain'd bridegroom took him such a cuff
That down fell priest and book, and book and priest!
'Now take them up', quoth he, 'if any list.'
    Tranio
160 What said the wench when he rose again?
    Gremio
Trembled and shook, for why he stamp'd and swore
As if the vicar meant to cozen him.
But after many ceremonies done
He calls for wine. 'A health', quoth he, as if
165 He had been aboard, carousing to his mates
After a storm; quaff'd off the muscadel
And threw the sops all in the sexton's face,
Having no other reason
But that his beard grew thin and hungerly
170 And seem'd to ask him sops as he was drinking.
This done, he took the bride about the neck
And kiss'd her lips with such a clamorous smack
That at the parting all the church did echo.
And I, seeing this, came thence for very shame,
175 And after me, I know, the rout is coming.
Such a mad marriage never was before!

157 *took . . . cuff*: gave him such a blow.

159 *if any list*: if anybody wants to.

161 *for why*: on account of which.
162 *cozen*: cheat.
163 *after . . . done*: when all the religious rites were finished.

165 *aboard*: on board ship.
    carousing: drinking healths.
166 *the muscadel*: At Elizabethan weddings it was traditional to offer pieces of cake ('sops') soaked in sweet white wine ('muscadel').
169 *hungerly*: sparsely, hungrily.
170 *ask him sops*: ask him for the sops.

175 *the rout*: the whole crowd of guests.

Music plays

Hark, hark! I hear the minstrels play.

Enter Petruchio, Katherina, Bianca, Hortensio *as*
Litio, Baptista, Grumio, *and others*

Petruchio

178 *pains*: concern.

179 *think*: expect.

180 *cheer*: food and drink.

181 *my haste . . . hence*: I am in a hurry to get away.

183 *will away*: will go away.

184 *must away*: must go away.

185 *Make it no wonder*: don't be surprised.

Gentlemen and friends, I thank you for your pains.
I know you think to dine with me today
180 And have prepar'd great store of wedding cheer,
But so it is, my haste doth call me hence,
And therefore here I mean to take my leave.
Baptista
Is't possible you will away tonight?
Petruchio
I must away today, before night come.
185 Make it no wonder; if you knew my business,
You would entreat me rather go than stay.
And, honest company, I thank you all
That have beheld me give away myself
To this most patient, sweet, and virtuous wife.
190 Dine with my father, drink a health to me,
For I must hence, and farewell to you all.
Tranio
Let us entreat you stay till after dinner.
Petruchio
It may not be.
Gremio
      Let me entreat you.
Petruchio
It cannot be.
Katherina
      Let me entreat you.
Petruchio
195 I am content.
Katherina
      Are you content to stay?
Petruchio
I am content you shall entreat me stay—
But yet not stay, entreat me how you can.

198 *horse*: As a plural form (like *sheep* and *deer*) *horse* was available until the 17th century.
199 *oats . . . horses*: Grumio's nonsense might be taken to mean that the feed was stronger than Petruchio's poor animals.

204 *You . . . green*: get away while your boots are fresh ('green').

206 *jolly . . . groom*: arrogant, miserable fellow.
207 *take it on you*: presume.
roundly: boldly.

209 *what . . . to do*: what has it to do with you.
210 *Father, be quiet*: Katherina anticipates an interruption from Baptista.
stay my leisure: wait until I am ready.
211 *now . . . work*: things are beginning to happen now.

217 *domineer*: riot.
218 *full measure*: all you can.
221 *look not big*: don't defy me; Petruchio speaks to the onlookers—who are making no resistance.
stare: look round wildly.
223–5 *She . . . anything*: Petruchio, while insisting on his legal rights to Katherina, seems to be accusing the company of covetousness.
223 *chattels*: moveable possessions.
224 *household-stuff*: furniture.

227 *bring mine action*: take legal proceedings against
he: man.

Katherina
Now, if you love me, stay.
Petruchio
                  Grumio, my horse!
Grumio
Ay, sir, they be ready—the oats have eaten the horses.
Katherina
200 Nay then,
Do what thou canst, I will not go today!
No, nor tomorrow—not till I please myself.
The door is open, sir, there lies your way;
You may be jogging whiles your boots are green.
205 For me, I'll not be gone till I please myself.
'Tis like you'll prove a jolly surly groom
That take it on you at the first so roundly.
Petruchio
O Kate, content thee; prithee be not angry.
Katherina
I will be angry. What hast thou to do?
210 —Father, be quiet. He shall stay my leisure.
Gremio
Ay, marry, sir, now it begins to work.
Katherina
Gentlemen, forward to the bridal dinner.
I see a woman may be made a fool
If she had not a spirit to resist.
Petruchio
215 They shall go forward, Kate, at thy command.
Obey the bride, you that attend on her.
Go to the feast, revel and domineer,
Carouse full measure to her maidenhead,
Be mad and merry—or go hang yourselves.
220 But for my bonny Kate, she must with me.
Nay, look not big, nor stamp, nor stare, nor fret;
I will be master of what is mine own.
She is my goods, my chattels; she is my house,
My household-stuff, my field, my barn,
225 My horse, my ox, my ass, my anything,
And here she stands. Touch her whoever dare,
I'll bring mine action on the proudest he
That stops my way in Padua. Grumio,

'I see a woman may be made a fool If she had not a spirit to resist.' (*3*, 2, 213–14). Josie Lawrence as Katherina and Michael Siberry as Petruchio, Royal Shakespeare Company, 1995.

Draw forth thy weapon—We are beset with thieves!
230 Rescue thy mistress, if thou be a man.
—Fear not, sweet wench, they shall not touch thee,
Kate;

232 *buckler*: defend, shield.

I'll buckler thee against a million!
[*Exeunt* Petruchio, Katherina, *and* Grumio
Baptista
Nay, let them go—a couple of quiet ones!
Gremio

234 *Went they not*: if they had not gone.

Went they not quickly, I should die with laughing.
Tranio
235 Of all mad matches never was the like.
Lucentio
Mistress, what's your opinion of your sister?
Bianca

237 *madly mated*: matched with a
madman.

That being mad herself, she's madly mated.
Gremio

238 *Kated*: matched with Kate.

I warrant him, Petruchio is Kated.
Baptista
Neighbours and friends, though bride and bridegroom
wants

239 *wants*: are missing.
240 *supply the places*: take their places.
241 *there wants no*: there is no lack of.
junkets: sweetmeats, delicacies.

240 For to supply the places at the table,
You know there wants no junkets at the feast.
[*To* Tranio] Lucentio, you shall supply the
bridegroom's place,

243 *room*: seat.

And let Bianca take her sister's room.
Tranio

244 *to bride it*: to act like a bride; Tranio
seems to step back into his assumed
role as the lover of Bianca, and
Baptista recognizes him as 'Lucentio'.

Shall sweet Bianca practise how to bride it?
Baptista
245 She shall, Lucentio. Come, gentlemen, let's go.
[*Exeunt*

ACT 4

Act 4 Scene 1
Grumio describes the journey home and
tells the servants how they must behave
when their new mistress arrives. Katherina,
exhausted and frightened, goes to bed—
and Petruchio explains his tactics for
taming a shrew.

1 *jades*: nags, weak horses.
2 *ways*: roads.
  rayed: muddied.
3 *am sent before*: have been sent
  ahead.
5 *a little . . . hot*: 'a small pot boils
  quickly' (proverbial); a little man is
  soon angered.
7 *come by*: find.
8 *blowing the fire*: fanning the embers.
9 *taller*: stronger (as well as bigger).
  take: catch.
10 *Curtis*: The name of an actor playing
  small parts in Shakespeare's company.

13 *no . . . run*: i.e. to get up speed.

16–17 *fire . . . water*: Grumio adapts a
  popular round, 'Scotland's burning
  . . . Fire, fire! Cast on water'.
18 *hot*: violent, quarrelsome.

20 *winter . . . beast*: The proverb is
  'Winter and wedlock tame both man
  and beast'.
21–2 *fellow Curtis*: Grumio allows Curtis
  to identify himself as his 'fellow'—and
  by implication a beast.

SCENE 1

Petruchio's country house: enter Grumio

Grumio
Fie, fie on all tired jades, on all mad masters, and all foul
ways! Was ever man so beaten? Was ever man so rayed?
Was ever man so weary? I am sent before to make a fire,
and they are coming after to warm them. Now were not
5 I a little pot and soon hot, my very lips might freeze to
my teeth, my tongue to the roof of my mouth, my heart
in my belly, ere I should come by a fire to thaw me. But
I with blowing the fire shall warm myself, for,
considering the weather, a taller man than I will take
10 cold. Holla, ho! Curtis!

Enter Curtis

Curtis
Who is that calls so coldly?
Grumio
A piece of ice. If thou doubt it, thou mayst slide from
my shoulder to my heel with no greater a run but my
head and my neck. A fire, good Curtis.
Curtis
15 Is my master and his wife coming, Grumio?
Grumio
O ay, Curtis, ay, and therefore fire, fire! Cast on no
water.
Curtis
Is she so hot a shrew as she's reported?
Grumio
She was, good Curtis, before this frost. But thou know'st
20 winter tames man, woman, and beast; for it hath tamed
my old master, and my new mistress, and myself, fellow
Curtis.

Curtis
Away, you three-inch fool, I am no beast!
Grumio
Am I but three inches? Why, thy horn is a foot, and so
25 long am I at the least. But wilt thou make a fire, or shall
I complain on thee to our mistress, whose hand—she
being now at hand—thou shalt soon feel, to thy cold
comfort, for being slow in thy hot office.
Curtis
I prithee, good Grumio, tell me, how goes the world?
Grumio
30 A cold world, Curtis, in every office but thine, and
therefore, fire. Do thy duty, and have thy duty, for my
master and mistress are almost frozen to death.
Curtis
There's fire ready, and therefore, good Grumio, the
news.
Grumio
35 Why, 'Jack boy, ho boy!' and as much news as wilt thou.
Curtis
Come, you are so full of cony-catching.
Grumio
Why, therefore fire, for I have caught extreme cold.
Where's the cook? Is supper ready, the house trimmed,
rushes strewed, cobwebs swept, the servingmen in their
40 new fustian, their white stockings, and every officer his
wedding garment on? Be the Jacks fair within, the Jills
fair without, the carpets laid, and everything in order?
Curtis
All ready, and therefore, I pray thee, news.
Grumio
First know my horse is tired, my master and mistress
45 fallen out.
Curtis
How?
Grumio
Out of their saddles into the dirt, and thereby hangs a
tale.
Curtis
Let's ha't, good Grumio.

23 *three-inch*: under-sized.

24 *horn*: a) cuckold's horn; b) penis; Grumio implies that he is big enough to have cuckolded Curtis.

27–8 *cold comfort*: discomfort.
28 *hot office*: job of making a fire.

29 *how goes the world*: what's the news.

31 *have thy duty*: take what is due to you.

35 *'Jack boy, ho boy!'*: Another popular song or catch.

36 *cony-catching*: trickery—with some play on Grumio's fondness for catches.

38 *trimmed*: tidied.
39 *rushes*: the normal floor covering.
40 *fustian*: coarse (and cheap) fabric, suitable for servingmen's livery.
41 *wedding garments*: These may be no more than tokens, like the carnations worn nowadays; but see Matthew 22:12.
Jacks . . . Jills: a) leather drinking-vessels and pewter mugs; b) male and female servants.
42 *without*: outside.
carpets: woollen table coverings.

47–8 *thereby hangs a tale*: there's a good story about that.

49 *ha't*: have it.

50 *Lend thine ear*: listen.

54 *sensible*: a) rational; b) capable of
   being felt.

56 *Imprimis*: first of all; Grumio attempts
   legal jargon.

58 *of*: on.

61 *crossed*: interrupted.

63 *miry*: muddy.
64 *bemoiled*: covered in mud.

70 *of worthy memory*: worth recording.
71 *unexperienced*: ignorant.

72 *By this reckoning*: from this account.
   more shrew: more of a shrew; the word
   is applicable to either sex.

74 *what*: why.

Grumio
50 Lend thine ear.
Curtis
Here.
Grumio
There.

He boxes Curtis's *ear*

Curtis
This 'tis to feel a tale, not to hear a tale.
Grumio
And therefore 'tis called a sensible tale; and this cuff was
55 but to knock at your ear and beseech listening. Now I
begin. *Imprimis* we came down a foul hill, my master
riding behind my mistress.
Curtis
Both of one horse?
Grumio
What's that to thee?
Curtis
60 Why, a horse.
Grumio
Tell thou the tale. But hadst thou not crossed me, thou
shouldst have heard how her horse fell, and she under
her horse; thou shouldst have heard in how miry a
place, how she was bemoiled, how he left her with the
65 horse upon her, how he beat me because her horse
stumbled, how she waded through the dirt to pluck him
off me, how he swore, how she prayed that never prayed
before, how I cried, how the horses ran away, how her
bridle was burst, how I lost my crupper—with many
70 things of worthy memory which now shall die in
oblivion, and thou return unexperienced to thy grave.
Curtis
By this reckoning he is more shrew than she.
Grumio
Ay, and that thou and the proudest of you all shall find
when he comes home. But what talk I of this? Call forth
75 Nathaniel, Joseph, Nicholas, Philip, Walter, Sugarsop

76 *and the rest*: Shakespeare probably did not know which, or how many, actors would be available to play these servingmen.
slickly: sleekly.
77 *blue coats*: normal servant uniform. *indifferent*: matching.
78 *curtsy . . . legs*: bend their left legs when they bow.
80 *kiss . . . hands*: i.e. in ceremonious greeting.

84 *countenance*: to pay respects to; Grumio, of course, wilfully misunderstands.

89 *credit*: honour; Grumio chooses to understand 'offer financial credit'.

90s.d. *four or five*: Shakespeare asks again—as at *4, 1, 76*—for whatever actors are available.

97 *spruce companions*: fine fellows.
98 *neat*: tidy.

and the rest. Let their heads be slickly combed, their blue coats brushed, and their garters of an indifferent knit. Let them curtsy with their left legs, and not presume to touch a hair of my master's horse-tail till
80 they kiss their hands. Are they all ready?

Curtis

They are.

Grumio

Call them forth.

Curtis

Do you hear, ho? You must meet my master to countenance my mistress.

Grumio

85 Why, she hath a face of her own.

Curtis

Who knows not that?

Grumio

Thou, it seems, that calls for company to countenance her.

Curtis

I call them forth to credit her.

Grumio

90 Why, she comes to borrow nothing of them.

Enter four or five Servingmen

Nathaniel

Welcome home, Grumio.

Philip

How now, Grumio.

Joseph

What, Grumio.

Nicholas

Fellow Grumio.

Nathaniel

95 How now, old lad.

Grumio

Welcome you; how now you; what you; fellow you; and thus much for greeting. Now, my spruce companions, is all ready, and all things neat?

100 *E'en at hand*: very close indeed.
    alighted: dismounted.
101 *Cock's passion*: God's (i.e. Christ's)
    suffering.

102 *at door*: to open the door.
103 *hold my stirrup*: i.e. to keep it steady
    whilst the rider dismounted.

107 *logger-headed*: block-headed;
    Petruchio has a fine command of
    abusive terms.
108 *regard*: respect.
    duty: obedience.

111 *peasant swain*: country oaf.
    whoreson: son of a whore.
    malthorse: heavy horse turning a
    treadmill to grind malt; the epitome of
    mindless drudgery.
112 *meet me in the park*: i.e. before the
    party arrived at the house.
115 *pumps . . . heel*: light shoes, whose
    heels should have been decorated
    with a pattern of small holes (pinked);
    Grumio is inventing excuses—in a
    manner (and in verse) which suggests
    that he is an accomplice in
    Petruchio's scheme.
116 *link*: torch, whose smoke could be
    used to darken the hat.
117 *sheathing*: being fitted with a sheath.
118 *fine*: properly dressed.

122–3 *Where . . . those—*: Petruchio sings
    an old ballad.

Nathaniel
All things is ready. How near is our master?
    Grumio
100 E'en at hand, alighted by this. And therefore be not—
    Cock's passion, silence! I hear my master.

Enter Petruchio *and* Katherina

    Petruchio
Where be these knaves? What, no man at door
To hold my stirrup, nor to take my horse?
Where is Nathaniel, Gregory, Philip?
    All Servingmen
105 Here! Here sir, here sir!
    Petruchio
'Here sir, here sir, here sir, here sir'!
You logger-headed and unpolish'd grooms!
What, no attendance? No regard? No duty?
Where is the foolish knave I sent before?
    Grumio
110 Here sir, as foolish as I was before.
    Petruchio
You peasant swain! You whoreson malthorse drudge!
Did I not bid thee meet me in the park
And bring along these rascal knaves with thee?
    Grumio
Nathaniel's coat, sir, was not fully made,
115 And Gabriel's pumps were all unpink'd i'th'heel.
There was no link to colour Peter's hat
And Walter's dagger was not come from sheathing.
There were none fine but Adam, Rafe, and Gregory;
The rest were ragged, old, and beggarly.
120 Yet, as they are, here are they come to meet you.
    Petruchio
Go, rascals, go, and fetch my supper in.
                              [*Exeunt* Servingmen
[*Sings*] Where is the life that late I led?
        Where are those—
Sit down, Kate, and welcome. Food, food, food, food!

Enter Servants *with supper*

125 *Why, when*: Petruchio is impatient.

127–8 *It was . . . way*: Another fragment of
song.
128 *walked*: walkèd.
129 *pluck*: pull.

130 *mend*: improve.

132 *Troilus*: a tragic lover of Greek legend,
and the hero of Shakespeare's *Troilus
and Cressida*.
133 *my cousin Ferdinand*: There is no
such character in the play.

137 *let it fall*: Perhaps Petruchio knocks
the basin of water out of the servant's
hands.

139 *beetle-headed*: A 'beetle' was a heavy
mallet.
flap-ear'd: with flapping ears (like a
donkey).
140 *have a stomach*: are hungry.
141 *give thanks*: say grace.

145 *dresser*: sideboard, serving-table.

125 Why, when, I say? Nay, good sweet Kate, be merry.
Off with my boots, you rogues, you villains! When?
[*Sings*] It was the friar of orders grey
        As he forth walked on his way—
Out, you rogue! You pluck my foot awry.
130 Take that!

He strikes the Servant

        And mend the plucking off the other.
Be merry, Kate. Some water here! What ho!

Enter one with water

Where's my spaniel Troilus? Sirrah, get you hence
And bid my cousin Ferdinand come hither—
                        [*Exit a* Servant
One, Kate, that you must kiss and be acquainted with.
135 Where are my slippers? Shall I have some water?
Come, Kate, and wash, and welcome heartily.
You whoreson villain! Will you let it fall?

He strikes the Servant

Katherina
Patience, I pray you. 'Twas a fault unwilling.
Petruchio
A whoreson, beetle-headed, flap-ear'd knave!
140 Come, Kate, sit down, I know you have a stomach.
Will you give thanks, sweet Kate, or else shall I?
What's this? Mutton?
First Servingman
                        Ay.
Petruchio
                                Who brought it?
Peter
                                        I.
Petruchio
'Tis burnt, and so is all the meat.
What dogs are these! Where is the rascal cook?
145 How durst you villains bring it from the dresser

147   *trenchers*: wooden plates.

And serve it thus to me that love it not?
There, take it to you, trenchers, cups and all!

He throws the food and dishes at them

148   *joltheads*: blockheads.

149   *be with you straight*: see to you at once.

You heedless joltheads and unmanner'd slaves!
What, do you grumble? I'll be with you straight.
[*Exeunt* Servants

Katherina

150   *disquiet*: distressed; Kate is already somewhat subdued.

150   I pray you, husband, be not so disquiet.
The meat was well, if you were so contented.

Petruchio

I tell thee, Kate, 'twas burnt and dried away,

153   *expressly*: especially.

154   *it engenders . . . anger*: It was generally thought that over-cooked meat produced an excess of the choleric humour, which caused anger.

156   *of ourselves*: naturally.

157   *it*: i.e. their choler.

159   *for company*: together.

And I expressly am forbid to touch it,
For it engenders choler, planteth anger;
155   And better 'twere that both of us did fast,
Since, of ourselves, ourselves are choleric,
Than feed it with such over-roasted flesh.
Be patient. Tomorrow't shall be mended,
And for this night we'll fast for company.
160   Come, I will bring thee to thy bridal chamber.   [*Exeunt*

Enter Servants *severally*

Nathaniel
Peter, didst ever see the like?
Peter
He kills her in her own humour.

162   *kills . . . humour*: beats her at her own game; Petruchio's bad temper is outdoing Katherina's temper.

Enter Curtis

Grumio
Where is he?
Curtis
In her chamber,

165   *of continency*: about self-control.

166   *rails*: shouts.
rates: scolds.
that: so that.

165   Making a sermon of continency to her,
And rails and swears and rates, that she, poor soul,
Knows not which way to stand, to look, to speak,
And sits as one new-risen from a dream.
Away, away, for he is coming hither.   [*Exeunt*

Enter Petruchio

Petruchio

170 Thus have I politicly begun my reign,
  And 'tis my hope to end successfully.
  My falcon now is sharp and passing empty,
  And till she stoop she must not be full-gorged,
  For then she never looks upon her lure.
175 Another way I have to man my haggard,
  To make her come and know her keeper's call,
  That is, to watch her, as we watch these kites
  That bate and beat and will not be obedient.
  She ate no meat today, nor none shall eat;
180 Last night she slept not, nor tonight she shall not.
  As with the meat, some undeserved fault
  I'll find about the making of the bed,
  And here I'll fling the pillow, there the bolster,
  This way the coverlet, another way the sheets.
185 Ay, and amid this hurly I intend
  That all is done in reverend care of her.
  And, in conclusion, she shall watch all night,
  And if she chance to nod I'll rail and brawl
  And with the clamour keep her still awake.
190 This is a way to kill a wife with kindness,
  And thus I'll curb her mad and headstrong humour.
  He that knows better how to tame a shrew,
  Now let him speak—'tis charity to show.   [*Exit*

Act 4 Scene 2
Hortensio, seeing Bianca's response to Lucentio's courtship, vows to marry a rich widow of his acquaintance. Biondello announces the arrival of a stranger, whom Tranio induces to impersonate Lucentio's father.

3 *bears . . . hand*: deceives me completely.

4 *satisfy*: convince.

5 *mark*: note.

6–7 *read*: a) study; b) teach.

7 *resolve me that*: answer that for me.

8 *profess*: practise.
The . . . Love: Ovid's *Ars Amatoria*, a witty poem which presents love as a science.

11 *Quick proceeders*: fast learners; Hortensio picks up the academic vocabulary, where 'proceed' = graduate from BA to MA.

12 *durst*: dare.

14 *despiteful*: cruel.

15 *wonderful*: incredible.

SCENE 2

Padua: Baptista's house. Enter Tranio *disguised as* Lucentio *and* Hortensio *disguised as* Litio

Tranio
Is't possible, friend Litio, that mistress Bianca
Doth fancy any other but Lucentio?
I tell you, sir, she bears me fair in hand.
    Hortensio
Sir, to satisfy you in what I have said,
5 Stand by, and mark the manner of his teaching.

They stand aside

Enter Bianca *and* Lucentio *disguised as* Cambio

Lucentio
Now mistress, profit you in what you read?
    Bianca
What, master, read you? First resolve me that.
    Lucentio
I read that I profess, *The Art to Love*.
    Bianca
And may you prove, sir, master of your art.
    Lucentio
10 While you, sweet dear, prove mistress of my heart.

They court

Hortensio
Quick proceeders, marry! Now tell me, I pray,
You that durst swear that your mistress Bianca
Lov'd none in the world so well as Lucentio.
    Tranio
O despiteful love, unconstant womankind!
15 I tell thee, Litio, this is wonderful.
    Hortensio
Mistake no more—I am not Litio,
Nor a musician as I seem to be,
But one that scorn to live in this disguise

For such a one as leaves a gentleman
20 And makes a god of such a cullion.
Know, sir, that I am call'd Hortensio.
>   **Tranio**
Signor Hortensio, I have often heard
Of your entire affection to Bianca,
And since mine eyes are witness of her lightness,
25 I will with you, if you be so contented,
Forswear Bianca and her love for ever.
>   **Hortensio**
See how they kiss and court! Signor Lucentio,
Here is my hand, and here I firmly vow
Never to woo her more, but do forswear her
30 As one unworthy all the former favours
That I have fondly flatter'd her withal.
>   **Tranio**
And here I take the like unfeigned oath
Never to marry with her though she would entreat.
Fie on her! See how beastly she doth court him.
>   **Hortensio**
35 Would all the world but he had quite forsworn!
For me, that I may surely keep mine oath,
I will be married to a wealthy widow
Ere three days pass, which hath as long lov'd me
As I have lov'd this proud disdainful haggard.
40 And so farewell, Signor Lucentio.
Kindness in women, not their beauteous looks,
Shall win my love; and so I take my leave,
In resolution as I swore before.

>   Tranio *joins* Lucentio *and* Bianca

>   **Tranio**
Mistress Bianca, bless you with such grace
45 As 'longeth to a lover's blessed case!
Nay, I have tane you napping, gentle love,
And have forsworn you with Hortensio.
>   **Bianca**
Tranio, you jest—but have you both forsworn me?
>   **Tranio**
Mistress, we have.

---

20 *cullion*: peasant.

23 *entire affection to*: sincere love for.
24 *lightness*: unfaithfulness.

31 *fondly*: foolishly.

32 *unfeigned*: unfeignèd.
33 *though . . . entreat*: even if she asked me to.
34 *beastly*: lasciviously; perhaps the lovers are kissing.
35 *Would . . . forsworn*: I wish everyone else had given her up (so that Bianca would be forced to marry her tutor).
37 *a wealthy widow*: This character seems to have been introduced only to provide three women (a traditional number) for the final scene.
39 *haggard*: wild hawk; Hortensio uses Petruchio's imagery.
41 *Kindness*: natural affection.

43 *In resolution*: quite determined.

45 *'longeth*: belongs.
blessed: blessèd.
case: situation.
46 *tane you napping*: caught you by surprise.

Lucentio

                    Then we are rid of Litio.

Tranio

50 I'faith, he'll have a lusty widow now

That shall be woo'd and wedded in a day.

Bianca

God give him joy!

Tranio

Ay, and he'll tame her.

Bianca

                    He says so, Tranio?

Tranio

Faith, he is gone unto the taming-school.

Bianca

55 The taming-school? What, is there such a place?

Tranio

Ay, mistress, and Petruchio is the master,

That teacheth tricks eleven and twenty long

To tame a shrew and charm her chattering tongue.

Enter Biondello

Biondello

O master, master, I have watch'd so long

60 That I am dog-weary, but at last I spied

An ancient angel coming down the hill

Will serve the turn.

Tranio

                    What is he, Biondello?

Biondello

Master, a marcantant, or a pedant,

I know not what, but formal in apparel,

65 In gait and countenance surely like a father.

Lucentio

And what of him, Tranio?

Tranio

If he be credulous and trust my tale,

I'll make him glad to seem Vincentio

And give assurance to Baptista Minola

70 As if he were the right Vincentio.

---

50 *lusty*: merry.

57 *eleven and twenty long*: just the job, the right ones (compare *1, 2, 31* note).
58 *charm*: put a spell on, silence.

60 *dog-weary*: tired out.
61 *ancient angel*: a heaven-sent old man.
62 *serve the turn*: be just right for our purpose.

63 *marcantant*: merchant; presumably Biondello mispronounces the Italian *mercatante*.
    pedant: teacher; the pedant was one of the stock characters of the *commedia dell'arte*.
65 *countenance*: appearance.
66 *And . . . him*: Lucentio still seems unsure of the plot; see *1, 1, 163* note.
67 *trust my tale*: believe what I tell him.
68 *seem*: pretend to be.

Take in your love, and then let me alone.

[*Exeunt* Lucentio *and* Bianca

Enter a Merchant

Merchant
God save you, sir.
   Tranio
                     And you, sir. You are welcome.
Travel you farre on or are you at the farthest?
   Merchant
Sir, at the farthest for a week or two,
75 But then up farther, and as far as Rome,
And so to Tripoli, if God lend me life.
   Tranio
What countryman, I pray?
   Merchant
                     Of Mantua.
   Tranio
Of Mantua, sir? Marry, God forbid!
And come to Padua careless of your life?
   Merchant
80 My life, sir? How, I pray? For that goes hard.
   Tranio
'Tis death for anyone in Mantua
To come to Padua. Know you not the cause?
Your ships are stay'd at Venice, and the duke,
For private quarrel 'twixt your duke and him,
85 Hath publish'd and proclaim'd it openly.
'Tis marvel—but that you are but newly come,
You might have heard it else proclaim'd about.
   Merchant
Alas, sir, it is worse for me than so.
For I have bills for money by exchange
90 From Florence, and must here deliver them.
   Tranio
Well, sir, to do you courtesy,
This will I do, and this I will advise you—
First tell me, have you ever been at Pisa?

---

73 *farre on*: any further.
   at the farthest: as far as you go.

76 *Tripoli*: a trading city on the North African coast.

77 *What countryman*: where do you come from.

80 *goes hard*: is a serious matter.

83 *Your ships*: ships sailing under the Mantuan flag; like Padua (see *1*, 1, 42 note), Mantua may also be thought of as a sea-port.
   stay'd: detained.
84 *For . . . quarrel*: because of a personal quarrel.
85 *publish'd*: declared.
86 *'Tis . . . come*: it's a wonder that you have only arrived so recently.
88 *than so*: than that.
89–90 *bills . . . Florence*: promissory notes from Florence to exchange for cash.
91 *do you courtesy*: do you a favour.

95 *Pisa . . . citizens*: A strange repetition
   of *1*, 1, 10.
   renowned: renownèd.
96 *one*: a certain.

101 *apple . . . oyster*: A proverbial
    comparison.
    and all one: never mind about that.

102 *extremity*: danger.

106 *credit*: position.
    undertake: assume.
107 *friendly*: as a friend.
108 *Look that*: see to it that.
    take upon you: do what is required of
    you.

111 *If . . . court'sy*: if you think I'm doing
    you a kindness.

112 *repute*: consider.

113 *patron*: saviour.

114 *make the matter good*: put this plan
    into action.
115 *by the way*: as we go along.
116 *look'd for*: expected.
117 *pass assurance*: make a formal
    agreement.

119 *circumstances*: details.

120 *becomes you*: i.e. is appropriate for
    your new identity (as Vincentio of
    Pisa).

Merchant
Ay, sir, in Pisa have I often been,
95 Pisa renowned for grave citizens.
Tranio
Among them know you one Vincentio?
Merchant
I know him not, but I have heard of him,
A merchant of incomparable wealth.
Tranio
He is my father, sir, and sooth to say,
100 In count'nance somewhat doth resemble you.
Biondello
[*Aside*] As much as an apple doth an oyster, and all
   one!
Tranio
To save your life in this extremity,
This favour will I do you for his sake—
And think it not the worst of all your fortunes
105 That you are like to Sir Vincentio—
His name and credit shall you undertake,
And in my house you shall be friendly lodg'd.
Look that you take upon you as you should—
You understand me, sir? So shall you stay
110 Till you have done your business in the city.
If this be court'sy, sir, accept of it.
Merchant
O sir, I do, and will repute you ever
The patron of my life and liberty.
Tranio
Then go with me to make the matter good.
115 This, by the way, I let you understand:
My father is here look'd for every day
To pass assurance of a dower in marriage
'Twixt me and one Baptista's daughter here.
In all these circumstances I'll instruct you.
120 Go with me to clothe you as becomes you.   [*Exeunt*

Act 4 Scene 3
Petruchio, aided by Grumio, persists with the 'taming' of Katherina until she is sufficiently docile to obey his every command.

2 *The more . . . appears*: the greater the wrong done to me, the worse his temper grows.

5 *Upon entreaty*: as soon as they ask. *present*: immediate.

9 *meat*: food.

11 *spites*: hurts. *wants*: things I lack.
12 *name*: pretence.
13 *As who*: like one who.
14 *present*: instant.
15 *repast*: nourishment.

17 *neat's foot*: ox foot or calf's foot.

18 *passing*: extremely.

19 *choleric*: causing choler; Grumio obviously knows Petruchio's plan.
20 *tripe*: the stomach lining of a cow or sheep.

22 *I cannot tell*: I'm not sure.

26 *let . . . rest*: forget the mustard.

SCENE 3

Petruchio's house: enter Katherina *and* Grumio

Grumio
No, no, forsooth, I dare not for my life!
 Katherina
The more my wrong, the more his spite appears.
What, did he marry me to famish me?
Beggars that come unto my father's door
5 Upon entreaty have a present alms;
If not, elsewhere they meet with charity.
But I, who never knew how to entreat,
Nor never needed that I should entreat,
Am starv'd for meat, giddy for lack of sleep,
10 With oaths kept waking, and with brawling fed.
And that which spites me more than all these wants,
He does it under name of perfect love,
As who should say, if I should sleep or eat
'Twere deadly sickness or else present death.
15 I prithee go and get me some repast—
I care not what, so it be wholesome food.
 Grumio
What say you to a neat's foot?
 Katherina
'Tis passing good. I prithee let me have it.
 Grumio
I fear it is too choleric a meat.
20 How say you to a fat tripe finely broil'd?
 Katherina
I like it well. Good Grumio, fetch it me.
 Grumio
I cannot tell, I fear 'tis choleric.
What say you to a piece of beef and mustard?
 Katherina
A dish that I do love to feed upon.
 Grumio
25 Ay, but the mustard is too hot a little.
 Katherina
Why then, the beef, and let the mustard rest.

'The poorest service is repaid with thanks, And so shall mine before you touch the meat.' (4, 3, 45–6). Michael Siberry as Petruchio and Josie Lawrence as Katherina, Royal Shakespeare Company, 1995.

Grumio
Nay then, I will not. You shall have the mustard,
Or else you get no beef of Grumio.
Katherina
Then both, or one, or anything thou wilt.
Grumio
30 Why then, the mustard without the beef.
Katherina
Go, get thee gone, thou false deluding slave

Beats him

That feed'st me with the very name of meat.
Sorrow on thee and all the pack of you
That triumph thus upon my misery!
35 Go, get thee gone, I say.

Enter Petruchio *and* Hortensio *with meat*

Petruchio
How fares my Kate? What, sweeting, all amort?
Hortensio
Mistress, what cheer?
Katherina
                                        Faith, as cold as can be.
Petruchio
Pluck up thy spirits; look cheerfully upon me.
Here, love, thou seest how diligent I am
40 To dress thy meat myself, and bring it thee.
I am sure, sweet Kate, this kindness merits thanks.
What, not a word? Nay then, thou lov'st it not,
And all my pains is sorted to no proof.
Here, take away this dish.
Katherina
                                        I pray you, let it stand.
Petruchio
45 The poorest service is repaid with thanks,
And so shall mine before you touch the meat.
Katherina
I thank you, sir.

32 *the very name*: the name and nothing else.

36 *sweeting*: sweetheart.
amort: depressed.

37 *what cheer*: how are you.
cold: poor; Katherina refers to the hospitality—'cheer'—of Petruchio's house.

38 *Pluck up*: lift up.

40 *dress*: prepare.

43 *pains*: trouble (treated as a singular noun).
is . . . proof: has been in vain.

44 *let it stand*: leave it where it is; Katherina's completion of Petruchio's half-line shows the sharpness of her hunger.
46 *mine*: my service.

48 *blame*: blameworthy, at fault.

49 *bear you company*: join you (in the meal); Hortensio, like Grumio, seems to be a party to Petruchio's scheme.

52 *apace*: without hesitation; Hortensio is probably trying to eat everything while Petruchio distracts Katherina's attention.

54 *revel it*: enjoy ourselves.
bravely: splendidly dressed.

55–8 *With . . . knav'ry*: Petruchio chants the items of fashionable clothing like a pedlar.

56 *farthingales*: hooped skirts.

57 *brav'ry*: fine clothes.
58 *knav'ry*: nonsense.
59 *stays*: awaits.
60 *deck*: adorn.
ruffling: decorated with ruffles.
63 *bespeak*: order.
64 *porringer*: little basin.
65 *lewd and filthy*: cheap and nasty.
66 *cockle*: cockle-shell.
67 *knack . . . trick*: knick-knack, trifle, piece of nonsense.
69 *doth fit the time*: is fashionable.

72 *in haste*: in a hurry, very soon.

Hortensio
Signor Petruchio, fie, you are to blame.
Come, Mistress Kate, I'll bear you company.
   Petruchio
50 [*Aside*] Eat it up all, Hortensio, if thou lov'st me—
[*To* Katherina] Much good do it unto thy gentle heart.
Kate, eat apace. And now, my honey love,
Will we return unto thy father's house
And revel it as bravely as the best,
55 With silken coats and caps, and golden rings,
With ruffs and cuffs and farthingales and things,
With scarves and fans and double change of brav'ry,
With amber bracelets, beads, and all this knav'ry.
What, hast thou dined? The tailor stays thy leisure,
60 To deck thy body with his ruffling treasure.

Enter Tailor

Come, tailor, let us see these ornaments.
Lay forth the gown.

Enter Haberdasher

               What news with you, sir?
   Haberdasher
Here is the cap your worship did bespeak.
   Petruchio
Why, this was moulded on a porringer—
65 A velvet dish! Fie, fie, 'tis lewd and filthy.
Why, 'tis a cockle or a walnut-shell,
A knack, a toy, a trick, a baby's cap.
Away with it! Come, let me have a bigger.
   Katherina
I'll have no bigger. This doth fit the time,
70 And gentlewomen wear such caps as these.
   Petruchio
When you are gentle you shall have one too,
And not till then.
   Hortensio
[*Aside*]   That will not be in haste.

73 *leave*: permission.
75 *endur'd me say*: let me speak.
78 *it*: i.e. her anger.
82 *custard-coffin*: pastry case for a baked custard.
83 *in that*: because.
86 *Thy gown*: Perhaps Petruchio (wilfully) mishears Katherina's 'none' in the preceding line.
87 *masking stuff*: fancy dress costume.
88 *demi-cannon*: small cannon. See illustration.

89 *up . . . carv'd*: slit open all over (to show a different colour underneath).
91 *censer*: incense-burner (perhaps used as air-freshener).
92 *a devil's name*: in the devil's name.
93 *like*: likely.
94 *bid*: bade, ordered.
95 *the time*: in the modern way.
96 *and did*: and so I did.
   be remember'd: can remember.
97 *mar*: spoil.
98 *hop me . . . home*: hop off home.
   kennel: street gutter.
100 *make . . . it*: do what you can with it.
102 *quaint*: elegant.
103 *Belike*: it seems.
   puppet: doll (easily manipulated in puppet-shows); but Petruchio pretends that Katherina was speaking to the Tailor.

Katherina
Why, sir, I trust I may have leave to speak,
And speak I will. I am no child, no babe.
75 Your betters have endur'd me say my mind,
And if you cannot, best you stop your ears.
My tongue will tell the anger of my heart,
Or else my heart concealing it will break,
And, rather than it shall, I will be free
80 Even to the uttermost, as I please, in words.
Petruchio
Why, thou say'st true—it is a paltry cap.
A custard-coffin, a bauble, a silken pie!
I love thee well in that thou lik'st it not.
Katherina
Love me or love me not, I like the cap,
85 And it I will have, or I will have none.
Petruchio
Thy gown? Why, ay. Come, tailor, let us see't.
                    [*Exit* Haberdasher
O mercy God! What masking stuff is here?
What's this—a sleeve? 'Tis like a demi-cannon.
What, up and down carv'd like an apple-tart?
90 Here's snip and nip and cut and slish and slash,
Like to a censer in a barber's shop.
Why, what a devil's name, tailor, call'st thou this?
Hortensio
[*Aside*] I see she's like to have neither cap nor gown.
Tailor
You bid me make it orderly and well,
95 According to the fashion and the time.
Petruchio
Marry, and did. But if you be remember'd,
I did not bid you mar it to the time.
Go, hop me over every kennel home,
For you shall hop without my custom, sir.
100 I'll none of it. Hence, make your best of it.
Katherina
I never saw a better-fashion'd gown,
More quaint, more pleasing, nor more commendable.
Belike you mean to make a puppet of me.

Petruchio
Why, true, he means to make a puppet of thee.
Tailor
105 She says your worship means to make a puppet of her.
Petruchio
O monstrous arrogance! Thou liest, thou thread, thou
    thimble,
Thou yard, three-quarters, half-yard, quarter, nail!
Thou flea, thou nit, thou winter-cricket thou!
Brav'd in mine own house with a skein of thread?
110 Away, thou rag, thou quantity, thou remnant!
Or I shall so bemete thee with thy yard
As thou shalt think on prating whilst thou liv'st.
I tell thee, I, that thou hast marr'd her gown.
Tailor
Your worship is deceiv'd. The gown is made
115 Just as my master had direction.
Grumio gave order how it should be done.
Grumio
I gave him no order; I gave him the stuff.
Tailor
But how did you desire it should be made?
Grumio
Marry, sir, with needle and thread.
Tailor
120 But did you not request to have it cut?
Grumio
Thou hast faced many things.
Tailor
I have.
Grumio
Face not me. Thou hast braved many men; brave not
me. I will neither be faced nor braved. I say unto thee, I
125 bid thy master cut out the gown, but I did not bid him
cut it to pieces. *Ergo*, thou liest.
Tailor
Why, here is the note of the fashion to testify.
Petruchio
Read it.
Grumio
The note lies in's throat if he say I said so.

106–10 *thou thread . . . remnant*: The
    tailor's trade attracted sarcastic
    remarks and charges of effeminacy.
107 *yard*: length of 92 centimetres;
    yardstick (= rod for measuring lengths
    of fabric).
    nail: one-sixteenth of a yard.
108 *nit*: egg of a louse.
    winter-cricket: thin-legged insect.
109 *Brav'd*: a) defied; b) smartly dressed
    (see 124 below).
110 *quantity*: fragment.
111 *bemete*: a) measure out; b) beat.
112 *As . . . liv'st*: so that you will think
    carefully before prattling for the rest
    of your life.

117 *stuff*: fabric.

121 *faced*: a) trimmed; b) outfaced.

126 *Ergo*: therefore; a legal term.

127 *note*: written order.

129 *lies in's throat*: is a downright lie.

130 *Imprimis*: first of all.
loose-bodied gown: loosely fitting gown; but Grumio pretends to interpret this as a dress for a loose-living woman.
132 *bottom*: bobbin.

135 *compassed*: circular.

136 *confess*: admit.

137 *trunk*: full, wide.

139 *curiously*: carefully, elaborately.

141 *Error i'th'bill*: mistaken charge; the phrase is legal jargon—a criminal charge would fail if there were any error in the formal indictment.
143 *prove upon*: prove against; Grumio is preparing for a fight.

145 *and . . . where*: if I had you in the right place; the Tailor means a court of law.

147 *for . . . straight*: ready to fight you now.
bill: a) order-note; b) billhook.
148 *mete-yard*: measuring-stick.
149 *odds*: chance (armed only with the piece of paper).

150 *for me*: as I like it.

152 *take . . . use*: take it away and let your master do what he can with it; but Grumio wilfully misunderstands.

Tailor
130 [*Reads*] '*Imprimis*, a loose-bodied gown—'
Grumio
Master, if ever I said 'loose-bodied gown', sew me in the skirts of it and beat me to death with a bottom of brown thread. I said 'a gown'.
Petruchio
Proceed.
Tailor
135 'With a small compassed cape.'
Grumio
I confess the cape.
Tailor
'With a trunk sleeve.'
Grumio
I confess two sleeves.
Tailor
'The sleeves curiously cut.'
Petruchio
140 Ay, there's the villainy.
Grumio
Error i'th'bill, sir, error i'th'bill! I commanded the sleeves should be cut out and sewed up again—and that I'll prove upon thee, though thy little finger be armed in a thimble.
Tailor
145 This is true that I say, and I had thee in place where thou should'st know it.
Grumio
I am for thee straight. Take thou the bill, give me thy mete-yard and spare not me.
Hortensio
God-a-mercy, Grumio, then he shall have no odds.
Petruchio
150 Well, sir, in brief, the gown is not for me.
Grumio
You are i'th'right, sir, 'tis for my mistress.
Petruchio
Go, take it up unto thy master's use.

155 *conceit*: meaning.

156 *deeper . . . for*: more serious than you imagine.
157 *use*: (sexual) purposes.

159 *say . . . paid*: In this carefully calculated outburst of temper, Petruchio still considers the feelings of the Tailor.

162 *no unkindness of*: no offence at.

165 *honest mean habiliments*: respectable everyday clothes.
166 *proud*: rich (because they have not wasted money).

169 *peereth*: can be seen through.
habit: clothing.
170 *jay*: a loud-voiced, chattering bird.
lark: a plain brown bird, valued for its singing.

173 *painted*: patterned.

175 *furniture*: equipment.
mean array: poor clothes.
176 *account'st*: consider.
lay it on me: blame me.
177 *frolic*: be merry.

183 *by dinner-time*: in time for the main meal, usually served before noon.

185 *supper-time*: time for the evening meal, served before 6 p.m.

Grumio
Villain, not for thy life! Take up my mistress' gown for
thy master's use?
Petruchio
155 Why, sir, what's your conceit in that?
Grumio
O sir, the conceit is deeper than you think for.
Take up my mistress' gown to his master's use?
O fie, fie, fie!
Petruchio
[*Aside*] Hortensio, say thou wilt see the tailor paid.
160 [*To* Tailor] Go, take it hence; be gone and say no more.
Hortensio
[*Aside*] Tailor, I'll pay thee for thy gown tomorrow,
Take no unkindness of his hasty words.
Away I say, commend me to thy master.   [*Exit* Tailor
Petruchio
Well, come, my Kate, we will unto your father's
165 Even in these honest mean habiliments.
Our purses shall be proud, our garments poor,
For 'tis the mind that makes the body rich,
And as the sun breaks through the darkest clouds,
So honour peereth in the meanest habit.
170 What, is the jay more precious than the lark
Because his feathers are more beautiful?
Or is the adder better than the eel
Because his painted skin contents the eye?
O no, good Kate; neither art thou the worse
175 For this poor furniture and mean array.
If thou account'st it shame, lay it on me,
And therefore frolic! We will hence forthwith
To feast and sport us at thy father's house.
[*To* Grumio] Go call my men, and let us straight to
     him,
180 And bring our horses unto Long-lane end,
There will we mount, and thither walk on foot.
Let's see, I think 'tis now some seven o'clock,
And well we may come there by dinner-time.
Katherina
I dare assure you, sir, 'tis almost two,
185 And 'twill be supper-time ere you come there.

Petruchio
It shall be seven ere I go to horse.
Look what I speak, or do, or think to do,
You are still crossing it. Sirs, let't alone.
I will not go today, and, ere I do,
190 It shall be what o'clock I say it is.
Hortensio
[*Aside*] Why so this gallant will command the sun.

[*Exeunt*

187 *Look what*: whatever.
188 *still*: always.
     crossing: contradicting.
     let't: leave it.
189 *ere I do*: before I go at all.
190 *what o'clock*: whatever time.

SCENE 4

Padua: outside Baptista*'s house. Enter* Tranio
disguised as Lucentio *and the* Merchant, *booted and*
bare headed, dressed like Vincentio

Tranio
Sir, this is the house. Please it you that I call?
Merchant
Ay, what else? And, but I be deceiv'd,
Signor Baptista may remember me
Near twenty years ago in Genoa
5 Where we were lodgers at the Pegasus.
Tranio
'Tis well. And hold your own, in any case,
With such austerity as 'longeth to a father.
Merchant
I warrant you.

Enter Biondello

              But, sir, here comes your boy;
'Twere good he were school'd.
Tranio
10 Fear you not him. Sirrah Biondello,
Now do your duty throughly, I advise you:
Imagine 'twere the right Vincentio.
Biondello
Tut, fear not me.
Tranio
But hast thou done thy errand to Baptista?

Act 4 Scene 4
The Merchant (pretending to be Lucentio's
father) discusses arrangements for Bianca's
marriage, and Lucentio makes plans to
elope.

0s.d. *booted . . . headed*: The Merchant
     is still dressed as a traveller, and has
     removed his hat in readiness for his
     introduction to Baptista.
1 *please . . . call*: do you wish me to call
     them.
2–5 *And . . . Pegasus*: The Merchant
     rehearses his role.
2 *but I be*: unless I am.
5 *Pegasus*: the winged horse of classical
     mythology, a popular inn sign.

THE PEGASUS

6 *'Tis . . . case*: well done—keep it up
     whatever happens.
7 *austerity*: gravity.
   'longeth: belongs to, is proper for.
8 *warrant*: promise.
9 *school'd*: told what to do.
11 *throughly*: perfectly.
   advise: warn.
12 *right*: real.

16 *look'd for*: expected.

17 *tall fellow*: good chap.
hold . . . drink: take that and buy
yourself a drink.

18 *Set . . . countenance*: assume an
appropriate expression.

21 *stand*: show yourself to be.
22 *patrimony*: inheritance.

23 *Soft*: steady.

25 *gather in*: collect.
26 *weighty cause*: important matter.

28 *for*: because of.

30 *stay*: delay.

32 *have him match'd*: let him get
married.
like: approve.
33 *agreement*: financial settlement.
35 *one consent*: in full agreement.
bestow'd: given in marriage.
36 *curious*: over-particular (about the
settlement).

39 *shortness*: brevity of speech.

42 *dissemble*: pretend.

45 *pass*: allow.

Biondello
15 I told him that your father was at Venice,
And that you look'd for him this day in Padua.
Tranio
Th'art a tall fellow; hold thee that to drink.

He gives him money

Enter Baptista *and* Lucentio *disguised as* Cambio

Here comes Baptista. Set your countenance, sir.
Signor Baptista, you are happily met.
20 Sir, this is the gentleman I told you of.
I pray you stand good father to me now:
Give me Bianca for my patrimony.
Merchant
Soft, son.
Sir, by your leave, having come to Padua
25 To gather in some debts, my son Lucentio
Made me acquainted with a weighty cause
Of love between your daughter and himself.
And—for the good report I hear of you,
And for the love he beareth to your daughter,
30 And she to him—to stay him not too long,
I am content, in a good father's care,
To have him match'd. And if you please to like
No worse than I, upon some agreement
Me shall you find ready and willing
35 With one consent to have her so bestow'd,
For curious I cannot be with you,
Signor Baptista, of whom I hear so well.
Baptista
Sir, pardon me in what I have to say.
Your plainness and your shortness please me well.
40 Right true it is your son Lucentio here
Doth love my daughter, and she loveth him—
Or both dissemble deeply their affections—
And therefore, if you say no more than this,
That like a father you will deal with him,
45 And pass my daughter a sufficient dower,

The match is made and all is done:
Your son shall have my daughter with consent.
    Tranio
I thank you, sir. Where, then, do you know best
We be affied and such assurance tane

49 *affied*: formally betrothed; see
   2, 1, 310–11 note.
50 *As . . . stand*: as shall confirm the
   agreement on both sides.

50 As shall with either part's agreement stand?
    Baptista
Not in my house, Lucentio, for you know
Pitchers have ears, and I have many servants.
Besides, old Gremio is heark'ning still,
And happily we might be interrupted.
    Tranio
55 Then at my lodging, and it like you.
There doth my father lie, and there this night
We'll pass the business privately and well.
Send for your daughter by your servant here.

52 *Pitchers . . . ears*: everybody can hear
   (proverbial); literally—'water-jugs have
   handles'.

He indicates Lucentio *and winks at him*

My boy shall fetch the scrivener presently.
60 The worst is this, that at so slender warning
You are like to have a thin and slender pittance.
    Baptista
It likes me well. Cambio, hie you home,
And bid Bianca make her ready straight,
And, if you will, tell what hath happened:
65 Lucentio's father is arrived in Padua,
And how she's like to be Lucentio's wife.
                        [*Exit* Lucentio
    Biondello
I pray the gods she may, with all my heart!
    Tranio
Dally not with the gods, but get thee gone.
                       [*Exit* Biondello
—Signor Baptista, shall I lead the way?
70 Welcome. One mess is like to be your cheer.
Come, sir, we will better it in Pisa.
    Baptista
I follow you.
                         [*Exeunt*

53 *heark'ning still*: always listening.
54 *happily*: perhaps.
56 *lie*: stay.
57 *pass*: transact.
59 *scrivener*: notary (to write out the
   agreement).
   presently: at once.
60 *slender warning*: short notice.
61 *You . . . pittance*: there probably won't
   be much to eat.
63 *make . . . straight*: get herself ready
   immediately.
64 *happened*: happenèd.

66s.d. *Exit Lucentio*: Lucentio, followed
   by Biondello, probably moves slightly
   downstage, out of Baptista's direct
   line of sight.

68 *Dally not*: don't waste time.

70 *One . . . cheer*: a single dish will
   probably be all the hospitality you will
   receive.
71 *better it*: improve things.

Enter Lucentio *disguised as* Cambio *and* Biondello

Biondello
Cambio!
Lucentio
What say'st thou, Biondello?
Biondello
75 You saw my master wink and laugh upon you?
Lucentio
Biondello, what of that?
Biondello
Faith, nothing—but 'has left me here behind to expound the meaning or moral of his signs and tokens.
Lucentio
I pray thee, moralize them.
Biondello
80 Then thus: Baptista is safe, talking with the deceiving father of a deceitful son.
Lucentio
And what of him?
Biondello
His daughter is to be brought by you to the supper.
Lucentio
And then?
Biondello
85 The old priest at Saint Luke's church is at your command at all hours.
Lucentio
And what of all this?
Biondello
I cannot tell, except they are busied about a counterfeit assurance. Take you assurance of her *cum privilegio ad*
90 *imprimendum solum.* To the church! Take the priest, clerk and some sufficient honest witnesses.
If this be not that you look for, I have no more to say,
But bid Bianca farewell for ever and a day.
Lucentio
Hear'st thou, Biondello?
Biondello
95 I cannot tarry. I knew a wench married in an afternoon as she went to the garden for parsley to stuff a rabbit.

77 *'has*: he has; once again, the servant explains the plot to his master (compare *1*, 1, 163 note, and *4*, 2, 66).
79 *moralize them*: interpret them.

80 *safe*: safely out of the way.

89 *Take you assurance*: make sure (with a pun on 'assurance' = legal settlement).
89–90 *cum . . . solum*: with exclusive right to print; a phrase used for licensing books.
91 *sufficient*: competent.
92 *look for*: are hoping for.

And so may you, sir; and so adieu, sir. My master hath
appointed me to go to Saint Luke's to bid the priest be
ready to come against you come with your appendix.
                                                    [*Exit*

Lucentio
100 I may and will, if she be so contented.
She will be pleas'd—then wherefore should I doubt?
Hap what hap may, I'll roundly go about her.
It shall go hard if Cambio go without her.   [*Exit*

SCENE 5

Padua: approaching Baptista's *house. Enter*
Petruchio, Katherina, Hortensio, *and* Servants

Petruchio
Come on, a God's name! Once more toward our
    father's.
Good Lord, how bright and goodly shines the moon!
    Katherina
The moon? The sun! It is not moonlight now.
    Petruchio
I say it is the moon that shines so bright.
    Katherina
5 I know it is the sun that shines so bright.
    Petruchio
Now, by my mother's son—and that's myself—
It shall be moon or star or what I list
Or e'er I journey to your father's house.
[*To* Servants] Go on and fetch our horses back again.
10 Evermore cross'd and cross'd, nothing but cross'd!
    Hortensio
Say as he says, or we shall never go.
    Katherina
Forward, I pray, since we have come so far.
And be it moon or sun or what you please;
And if you please to call it a rush-candle,
15 Henceforth I vow it shall be so for me.
    Petruchio
I say it is the moon.

Marginal notes (left column):

99 *against you come*: in preparation for
    your coming.
    appendix: appendage—i.e. Bianca;
    Biondello continues his printing
    metaphors.
102 *Hap . . . may*: whatever may happen
    (proverbial).
    roundly . . . her: tackle her boldly (a
    naval metaphor).

Act 4 Scene 5
Petruchio and Katherina are returning to
Padua, accompanied by Hortensio, when
they encounter an old man—the real
Vincentio.

1 *a*: in.

7 *list*: like.

8 *Or e'er*: before.

9 *fetch . . . again*: Perhaps, having
    travelled 'so far' (line 12), they are
    walking to rest their horses.

14 *rush-candle*: cheap candle made from
    a rush dipped in grease (giving very
    poor light).

'I say it is the moon that shines so bright.' (4, 5, 4). Sinead Cusack as Katherina, Ian Talbot as Hortensio, Pete Postlethwaite as Grumio, and Alun Armstrong as Petruchio, Royal Shakespeare Company, 1982.

Katherina

               I know it is the moon.

Petruchio

Nay then you lie, it is the blessed sun.

Katherina

Then God be bless'd, it is the blessed sun.

But sun it is not, when you say it is not,

20 And the moon changes even as your mind.

What you will have it nam'd, even that it is,

And so it shall be so for Katherine.

Hortensio

[*Aside*] Petruchio, go thy ways. The field is won.

Petruchio

Well, forward, forward! Thus the bowl should run

25 And not unluckily against the bias.

Enter Vincentio

But soft, company is coming here.

[*To* Vincentio] Good morrow, gentle mistress, where

    away?

Tell me, sweet Kate, and tell me truly too,

Hast thou beheld a fresher gentlewoman?

30 Such war of white and red within her cheeks!

What stars do spangle heaven with such beauty

As those two eyes become that heavenly face?

Fair lovely maid, once more good day to thee.

Sweet Kate, embrace her for her beauty's sake.

Hortensio

35 [*Aside*] A will make the man mad, to make the woman

of him.

Katherina

Young budding virgin, fair and fresh and sweet,

Whither away, or where is thy abode?

Happy the parents of so fair a child!

40 Happier the man whom favourable stars

Allots thee for his lovely bedfellow.

Petruchio

Why, how now, Kate! I hope thou art not mad.

This is a man—old, wrinkled, faded, wither'd—

And not a maiden, as thou say'st he is.

17–18 *blessed*: blessèd.

20 *even . . . mind*: just as your mind changes; although she is submissive, Katherina still has spirit to suggest that Petruchio's mind is affected by changes of the moon—that he is a 'lunatic'.

23 *go thy ways*: well done, carry on.

24–5 *the bowl . . . bias*: In the game of bowls, one side of the bowl is weighted—with a 'bias'—to give a natural curving path; Petruchio is saying that Katherina is no longer behaving unnaturally ('unluckily').

26 *soft*: wait a moment.

27 *where away*: where are you going.

29 *fresher*: more youthful.

30–2 *Such . . . face*: Petruchio speaks the language of romantic love poetry.

35 *A*: he.
make the woman: make him play a woman's part.

40 *favourable stars*: a happy fate.

Katherina

45 Pardon, old father, my mistaking eyes
   That have been so bedazzled with the sun
   That everything I look on seemeth green.
   Now I perceive thou art a reverend father.
   Pardon, I pray thee, for my mad mistaking.

   Petruchio

50 Do, good old grandsire, and withal make known
   Which way thou travellest—if along with us
   We shall be joyful of thy company.

   Vincentio

   Fair sir, and you, my merry mistress,
   That with your strange encounter much amaz'd me,
55 My name is call'd Vincentio, my dwelling Pisa,
   And bound I am to Padua, there to visit
   A son of mine which long I have not seen.

   Petruchio

   What is his name?

   Vincentio

                        Lucentio, gentle sir.

   Petruchio

   Happily met—the happier for thy son.
60 And now by law as well as reverend age
   I may entitle thee my loving father.
   The sister to my wife, this gentlewoman,
   Thy son by this hath married. Wonder not,
   Nor be not griev'd. She is of good esteem,
65 Her dowry wealthy, and of worthy birth;
   Beside, so qualified as may beseem
   The spouse of any noble gentleman.
   Let me embrace with old Vincentio,
   And wander we to see thy honest son,
70 Who will of thy arrival be full joyous.

   Vincentio

   But is this true, or is it else your pleasure,
   Like pleasant travellers, to break a jest
   Upon the company you overtake?

   Hortensio

   I do assure thee, father, so it is.

---

47 *green*: in colour; *also* young.
48 *reverend*: to be revered.

56 *bound I am*: I am going.

61 *entitle*: address you with the title.

63 *by this*: by this time; Petruchio and
   Hortensio should not know this yet—
   but the play has many such loose
   ends.
64 *esteem*: reputation.
66 *so qualified*: with such good qualities.
   beseem: be appropriate for.

69 *wander we*: let's travel on.
70 *of*: at.

72 *pleasant*: light-hearted.
   break a jest: play a trick.

Petruchio

75 Come, go along and see the truth hereof,
For our first merriment hath made thee jealous.

[Exeunt all but Hortensio

76 *merriment*: joking.
jealous: suspicious.
77 *put me in heart*: given me
encouragement.
78 *Have to*: forward to, now for.
froward: obstinate.
79 *untoward*: intractable—equally
obstinate.

Hortensio

Well, Petruchio, this has put me in heart!
Have to my widow, and if she be froward,
Then hast thou taught Hortensio to be untoward.

[Exit

Act 5 Scene 1
Lucentio and Bianca elope, and Petruchio brings Katherina back to Padua—along with the real Vincentio.

Os.d. *Gremio . . . before*: This unusual stage direction seems to indicate that the suspicious Gremio should come on stage first, apparently expecting to meet Bianca's Latin teacher, and lurking unseen to hear what is happening.

4 *see . . . back*: I'll wait till you are safely married.

6 *Cambio*: Gremio has not recognized Lucentio without his disguise.

8 *My father's*: i.e. Baptista's house. *bears more toward*: is more in the direction of.
9 *must I*: must I go.
10 *You . . . drink*: you must have a drink.
11 *I think I shall*: I'm sure I shall be able to.
12 *some . . . toward*: some good entertainment can be expected.

13 *within*: inside.

SCENE 1

Padua: a street. Enter Biondello, Lucentio *as himself, and* Bianca. Gremio *is out before*

Biondello
Softly and swiftly, sir, for the priest is ready.
    Lucentio
I fly, Biondello. But they may chance to need thee at home; therefore leave us.   [*Exit* Lucentio *with* Bianca
    Biondello
Nay, faith, I'll see the church a'your back, and then come
5 back to my master's as soon as I can.   [*Exit*
    Gremio
I marvel Cambio comes not all this while.

Enter Petruchio, Katherina, Vincentio, Grumio, *with* Attendants

    Petruchio
Sir, here's the door, this is Lucentio's house.
My father's bears more toward the market-place;
Thither must I, and here I leave you, sir.
    Vincentio
10 You shall not choose but drink before you go.
I think I shall command your welcome here,
And by all likelihood some cheer is toward.

He knocks

    Gremio
They're busy within. You were best knock louder.

Merchant looks out of the window

14 *as he*: as if he.

22 *leave frivolous circumstances*: forget about minor details.

25 *from Mantua*: The Folio text has 'from Padua', which is clearly wrong; perhaps the Merchant betrays himself by giving his own address.

30 *flat*: downright.

31 *a means*: he means.
    cozen: cheat.
32 *under my countenance*: by impersonating me.

34 *good shipping*: all success.

35–6 *brought to nothing*: utterly ruined.

37 *crack-hemp*: A term of abuse, referring to one fit only for hanging, who would stretch the hempen rope on the gallows.

Merchant
What's he that knocks as he would beat down the gate?
Vincentio
15 Is Signor Lucentio within, sir?
Merchant
He's within, sir, but not to be spoken withal.
Vincentio
What if a man bring him a hundred pound or two to make merry withal?
Merchant
Keep your hundred pounds to yourself. He shall need
20 none so long as I live.
Petruchio
Nay, I told you your son was well beloved in Padua. Do you hear, sir? To leave frivolous circumstances, I pray you tell Signor Lucentio that his father is come from Pisa and is here at the door to speak with him.
Merchant
25 Thou liest. His father is come from Mantua and here looking out at the window.
Vincentio
Art thou his father?
Merchant
Ay, sir, so his mother says, if I may believe her.
Petruchio
[*To* Vincentio] Why, how now, gentleman! Why, this is
30 flat knavery, to take upon you another man's name.
Merchant
Lay hands on the villain. I believe a means to cozen somebody in this city under my countenance.

Enter Biondello

Biondello
[*Aside*] I have seen them in the church together—God send 'em good shipping! But who is here? Mine old
35 master, Vincentio! Now we are undone and brought to nothing!
Vincentio
Come hither, crack-hemp.

38 *choose*: i.e. whether to come or go
   (= don't order me around).

Biondello
I hope I may choose, sir.
   Vincentio
Come hither, you rogue! What, have you forgot me?
   Biondello
40 Forgot you? No, sir. I could not forget you, for I never
saw you before in all my life.
   Vincentio
What, you notorious villain! Didst thou never see thy
master's father, Vincentio?
   Biondello
What, my old worshipful old master? Yes, marry, sir, see
45 where he looks out of the window.
   Vincentio
Is't so indeed?

He beats Biondello

Biondello
Help! Help! Help! Here's a madman will murder me!
                                             [*Exit*
   Merchant
Help, son! Help, Signor Baptista!
                              [*Exit from the window*
   Petruchio
Prithee, Kate, let's stand aside and see the end of this
50 controversy.

They stand aside

Enter Merchant *below with* Servants, Baptista, *and*
Tranio *disguised as* Lucentio

   Tranio
Sir, what are you that offer to beat my servant?
   Vincentio
What am I, sir? Nay, what are you, sir? O immortal gods!
O fine villain! A silken doublet, a velvet hose, a scarlet
cloak, and a copatain hat! O I am undone, I am undone!
55 While I play the good husband at home my son and my
servant spend all at the university.

51 *offer*: presume.
53 *a velvet hose*: pair of velvet breeches.
54 *a copatain hat*: See illustration; such
   hats were not to be worn by servants.

55 *play . . . husband*: manage my money
   carefully.

Tranio
How now, what's the matter?
    Baptista
What, is the man a lunatic?
    Tranio
Sir, you seem a sober ancient gentleman by your habit,
60 but your words show you a madman. Why, sir, what
'cerns it you if I wear pearl and gold? I thank my good
father, I am able to maintain it.
    Vincentio
Thy father? O villain! He is a sail-maker in Bergamo.
    Baptista
You mistake, sir; you mistake, sir. Pray, what do you
65 think is his name?
    Vincentio
His name? As if I knew not his name! I have brought
him up ever since he was three years old, and his name
is Tranio.
    Merchant
Away, away, mad ass! His name is Lucentio and he is
70 mine only son, and heir to the lands of me, Signor
Vincentio.
    Vincentio
Lucentio? O, he hath murdered his master! Lay hold on
him, I charge you in the duke's name. O my son, my
son! Tell me, thou villain, where is my son Lucentio?
    Tranio
75 Call forth an officer.

Enter an Officer

Carry this mad knave to the jail. Father Baptista, I
charge you see that he be forthcoming.
    Vincentio
Carry me to jail?
    Gremio
Stay, officer. He shall not go to prison.
    Baptista
80 Talk not, Signor Gremio. I say he shall go to prison.

59 *sober ancient*: respectable old.
    by your habit: to judge by your clothes.
60-1 *what . . . you*: what concern is it of yours.
62 *maintain*: afford.

63 *Bergamo*: an inland town of Northern Italy, traditionally the home of Harlequin, the intriguing comic servant of the *commedia dell'arte*.

77 *forthcoming*: brought to trial.

81 *cony-catched*: cheated, made a fool of.

Gremio
Take heed, Signor Baptista, lest you be cony-catched in this business. I dare swear this is the right Vincentio.
Merchant
Swear, if thou dar'st.
Gremio
Nay, I dare not swear it.

84 *I dare not*: Gremio's courage deserts him.

Tranio
85 Then thou wert best say that I am not Lucentio.
Gremio
Yes, I know thee to be Signor Lucentio.
Baptista
Away with the dotard, to the jail with him!

87 *dotard*: imbecile.

Vincentio
Thus strangers may be haled and abused. O monstrous villain!

88 *haled*: dragged about.
abused: misused.

Enter Biondello, Lucentio, *and* Bianca

Biondello
90 O, we are spoiled, and yonder he is! Deny him, forswear him, or else we are all undone.
                    [*Exeunt* Biondello, Tranio, *and* Merchant,
                                        as fast as may be

90 *spoiled*: ruined.

Lucentio
Pardon, sweet father.

Lucentio *and* Bianca *kneel*

Vincentio
                              Lives my sweet son?
Bianca
Pardon, dear father.
Baptista
                              How hast thou offended?
Where is Lucentio?
Lucentio
                              Here's Lucentio,
95 Right son to the right Vincentio,
That have by marriage made thy daughter mine
While counterfeit supposes blear'd thine eyne.

97 *supposes*: suppositions; in this word, Shakespeare alludes to the narrative from which he took the story of Bianca and Lucentio, George Gascoigne's *Supposes* (which was a translation of Ariosto's *I Suppositi*).
blear'd thine eyne: dimmed your eyes.

Gremio
Here's packing, with a witness, to deceive us all!
Vincentio
Where is that damned villain, Tranio,

100 That fac'd and brav'd me in this matter so?
Baptista
Why, tell me, is not this my Cambio?
Bianca
Cambio is chang'd into Lucentio.
Lucentio
Love wrought these miracles. Bianca's love
Made me exchange my state with Tranio

105 While he did bear my countenance in the town,
And happily I have arriv'd at the last
Unto the wished haven of my bliss.
What Tranio did, myself enforc'd him to;
Then pardon him, sweet father, for my sake.
Vincentio

110 I'll slit the villain's nose that would have sent me to the
jail!
Baptista
But do you hear, sir? Have you married my daughter
without asking my good will?
Vincentio
Fear not, Baptista, we will content you. Go to. But I will

115 in to be revenged for this villainy.   [*Exit*
Baptista
And I, to sound the depth of this knavery.   [*Exit*
Lucentio
Look not pale, Bianca, thy father will not frown.
                      [*Exeunt* Lucentio *and* Bianca
Gremio
My cake is dough, but I'll in among the rest,
Out of hope of all but my share of the feast.   [*Exit*
Katherina

120 Husband, let's follow, to see the end of this ado.
Petruchio
First kiss me, Kate, and we will.
Katherina
What in the midst of the street?

Petruchio

What, art thou ashamed of me?

Katherina

No sir, God forbid—but ashamed to kiss.

Petruchio

125 Why then, let's home again.

[*To* Grumio] Come, sirrah, let's away.

Katherina

Nay, I will give thee a kiss.

She kisses him

Now pray thee, love, stay.

Petruchio

Is not this well? Come, my sweet Kate,

130 Better once than never, for never too late.   [*Exeunt*

---

128 *Now . . . stay*: Katherina calls Petruchio 'love' for the first time—and perhaps shows the beginning of true harmony when she completes his rhyme.

130 *Better . . . late*: Petruchio combines two proverbs, 'Better late than never' and 'It is never too late to mend'.

Act 5 Scene 2
The three married couples enjoy an after-dinner conversation, and the husbands place bets on the obedience of their wives.

Os.d. *banquet*: dessert course of fruit, sweets, and wine.

1 *though long*: only after a long time.
  jarring: discordant.
  agree: are in harmony.
3 *scapes*: escapes.
  overblown: blown over, passed away.

5 *kindness*: courtesy; *and* kinship.

9 *close . . . up*: finish off our meal.
10 *great good cheer*: splendid reception.

SCENE 2

Baptista's house: the wedding feast. Enter Baptista, Vincentio, Gremio, *the* Merchant, Lucentio *and* Bianca, Hortensio *and the* Widow, Petruchio *and* Katherina, Tranio, Biondello *and* Grumio *with* Servingmen *bringing in a banquet*

Lucentio

At last, though long, our jarring notes agree,
And time it is when raging war is done
To smile at scapes and perils overblown.
My fair Bianca, bid my father welcome,
5 While I with selfsame kindness welcome thine.
Brother Petruchio, sister Katherina,
And thou Hortensio, with thy loving widow,
Feast with the best, and welcome to my house.
My banquet is to close our stomachs up
10 After our great good cheer. Pray you, sit down,
For now we sit to chat as well as eat.

Petruchio

Nothing but sit and sit, and eat and eat!

13 *Padua . . . kindness*: this is the usual hospitality in Padua.

14 *kind*: a) natural; b) affectionate.

15 *would*: wish.

16 *for my life*: upon my life.
fears: is frightened of; but the Widow misunderstands.
17 *afeard*: scared.

18 *sensible*: a) sensitive; b) intelligent.

20 *He . . . round*: The Widow's proverb implies that Petruchio must be afraid of Katherina.
21 *Roundly*: smartly.

22 *conceive*: a) understand; b) become pregnant.

24 *conceives her tale*: intends her meaning.

25 *mended*: saved.

28 *shrew*: The modern equivalent insult would be 'bitch'.
29 *his*: his own—i.e. Petruchio's.

31 *mean*: a) cheap; b) intend;
c) moderate.

32 *respecting you*: a) compared to you;
b) where you are concerned.

Baptista
Padua affords this kindness, son Petruchio.
   Petruchio
Padua affords nothing but what is kind.
   Hortensio
15 For both our sakes I would that word were true.
   Petruchio
Now, for my life, Hortensio fears his widow!
   Widow
Then never trust me if I be afeard.
   Petruchio
You are very sensible, and yet you miss my sense:
I mean Hortensio is afeard of you.
   Widow
20 He that is giddy thinks the world turns round.
   Petruchio
Roundly replied.
   Katherina
            Mistress, how mean you that?
   Widow
Thus I conceive by him.
   Petruchio
Conceives by me! How likes Hortensio that?
   Hortensio
My widow says, thus she conceives her tale.
   Petruchio
25 Very well mended. Kiss him for that, good widow.
   Katherina
'He that is giddy thinks the world turns round.'
I pray you tell me what you meant by that.
   Widow
Your husband, being troubl'd with a shrew,
Measures my husband's sorrow by his woe—
30 And now you know my meaning.
   Katherina
A very mean meaning.
   Widow
            Right, I mean you.
   Katherina
And I am mean indeed, respecting you.

33 *To her*: The husbands urge on their wives as though they were at a prize-fight—and then lay bets on the outcome.

35 *put her down*: defeat the Widow.

36 *my office*: my job (as a husband).

37 *ha' to thee*: here's to you.

39 *butt together*: bang their heads together (like young cattle).

40–1 *Head . . . horn*: Bianca's bawdy wordplay is surprising—but helps to prepare the audience for her subsequent behaviour.

40 *butt*: tail, bottom.
An . . . body: a quick-thinking person.

41 *head and horn*: a head with a cuckold's horn.

42 *awaken'd you*: Vincentio notes Bianca's sudden arousal.

45 *Have at you*: be prepared for.

46 *bird*: target.
shift: change.

48 *You . . . all*: The polite remark from a hostess as she leads the ladies out.

49 *prevented me*: got there before me; Petruchio concedes defeat.
Signor Tranio: For a moment Tranio becomes a social equal with the other gentlemen.

52 *slipp'd*: unleashed.

54 *swift*: quick-witted.
somewhat currish: rather more like a mongrel (than a greyhound).

Petruchio
To her, Kate!
Hortensio
To her, widow!
Petruchio
35 A hundred marks my Kate does put her down.
Hortensio
That's my office.
Petruchio
Spoke like an officer. Ha' to thee, lad.

He drinks to Hortensio

Baptista
How likes Gremio these quick-witted folks?
Gremio
Believe me, sir, they butt together well.
Bianca
40 Head and butt! An hasty-witted body
Would say your head and butt were head and horn.
Vincentio
Ay, mistress bride, hath that awaken'd you?
Bianca
Ay, but not frighted me; therefore I'll sleep again.
Petruchio
Nay, that you shall not. Since you have begun,
45 Have at you for a bitter jest or two.
Bianca
Am I your bird? I mean to shift my bush,
And then pursue me as you draw your bow.
You are welcome all.
              [*Exeunt* Bianca, Katherina, *and* Widow
Petruchio
She hath prevented me. Here, Signor Tranio,
50 This bird you aim'd at, though you hit her not—
Therefore a health to all that shot and miss'd.
Tranio
O sir, Lucentio slipp'd me like his greyhound,
Which runs himself and catches for his master.
Petruchio
A good swift simile, but something currish.

Tranio

55 'Tis well, sir, that you hunted for yourself—
'Tis thought your deer does hold you at a bay.

Baptista

O, O, Petruchio! Tranio hits you now.

Lucentio

I thank thee for that gird, good Tranio.

Hortensio

Confess! Confess! Hath he not hit you here?

Petruchio

60 A has a little gall'd me, I confess,
And as the jest did glance away from me,
'Tis ten to one it maim'd you two outright.

Baptista

Now in good sadness, son Petruchio,
I think thou hast the veriest shrew of all.

Petruchio

65 Well, I say no, and therefore, Sir Assurance,
Let's each one send unto his wife
And he whose wife is most obedient
To come at first when he doth send for her
Shall win the wager which we will propose.

Hortensio

70 Content. What's the wager?

Lucentio

                        Twenty crowns.

Petruchio

Twenty crowns?
I'll venture so much of my hawk or hound,
But twenty times so much upon my wife.

Lucentio

A hundred then.

Hortensio

              Content.

Petruchio

                    A match! 'Tis done.

Hortensio

75 Who shall begin?

Lucentio

              That will I.
Go, Biondello, bid your mistress come to me.

---

56 *deer*: Tranio puns on 'deer' and 'dear'; the stag is said to be 'at bay' when it turns and holds off the hounds.

58 *gird*: thrust.

60 *A*: he.
gall'd: touched.
61 *glance away*: bounce off.
62 *maim'd*: wounded.

63 *good sadness*: quite seriously.
64 *veriest*: truest.

65 *Sir Assurance*: An ironic form of address to the over-confident boaster[s].

72 *of*: on.

Biondello

I go.   [*Exit*

Baptista

78 *be your half*: share the bet with you.

Son, I'll be your half Bianca comes.

Lucentio

I'll have no halves; I'll bear it all myself.

Enter Biondello

80 How now, what news?

Biondello

                                        Sir, my mistress sends you word

That she is busy, and she cannot come.

Petruchio

How? 'She's busy and she cannot come'!

Is that an answer?

Gremio

83 *kind*: a) natural, appropriate; b) polite.

                                        Ay, and a kind one too.

Pray God, sir, your wife send you not a worse.

Petruchio

85 I hope better.

Hortensio

Sirrah Biondello, go and entreat my wife

To come to me forthwith.   [*Exit* Biondello

Petruchio

                                        O ho, 'entreat' her!

88 *must needs*: is sure to.

Nay then, she must needs come.

Hortensio

                                        I am afraid, sir,

Do what you can, yours will not be entreated.

Enter Biondello

90 Now, where's my wife?

Biondello

91 *you have . . . hand*: you're playing
    some funny trick.

She says you have some goodly jest in hand.

She will not come. She bids you come to her.

Petruchio

Worse and worse! 'She will not come'! O vile,

Intolerable, not to be endur'd!

95 Sirrah Grumio, go to your mistress.
    Say I command her come to me.   [*Exit* Grumio
        Hortensio
    I know her answer.
        Petruchio
                        What?
        Hortensio
                                She will not.
        Petruchio
98 *there an end*: that's all there is to it. The fouler fortune mine, and there an end.

    Enter Katherina

        Baptista
99 *by my holidame*: by all that I hold   Now, by my holidame, here comes Katherina!
    sacred.   **Katherina**
100 What is your will, sir, that you send for me?
        Petruchio
    Where is your sister, and Hortensio's wife?
        Katherina
102 *conferring*: gossiping.   They sit conferring by the parlour fire.
        Petruchio
    Go fetch them hither. If they deny to come,
104 *Swinge me . . . forth*: drive them out   Swinge me them soundly forth unto their husbands.
    (Petruchio's words suggest the use of
    physical force).   105 Away, I say, and bring them hither straight.
                                                    [*Exit* Katherina
        Lucentio
    Here is a wonder, if you talk of a wonder.
        Hortensio
107 *I . . . bodes*: Hortensio suspects that And so it is. I wonder what it bodes.
    this phenomenal behaviour may prove   **Petruchio**
    ominous.   Marry, peace it bodes, and love, and quiet life,
109 *awful*: commanding great respect.   An awful rule and right supremacy
    right: proper.
110 *what not that's*: everything else that   110 And, to be short, what not that's sweet and happy.
    is.   **Baptista**
111 *fair befall thee*: good luck to you,   Now fair befall thee, good Petruchio!
    congratulations.   The wager thou hast won, and I will add
                                              Unto their losses twenty thousand crowns,
113 *their losses*: i.e. the money that   Another dowry to another daughter,
    Lucentio and Hortensio have lost to
    Petruchio.
115 *as . . . been*: into a different person. 115 For she is chang'd, as she had never been.

117 *show more sign*: give more evidence.

118 *new-built*: new found; the repetition of 'obedience' in this line may be due to a printer's error (Shakespeare does not usually repeat himself without good reason).

119 *froward*: disobedient.

121 *becomes you not*: doesn't suit you.

122 *bauble*: piece of nonsense.
throw it under foot: stamp on it.

124 *brought . . . pass*: forced to do such a silly thing.

129 *laying*: laying a bet.

136–79 Katherina's speech forms the climax of the play, articulating many Elizabethan commonplaces about marriage, yet appearing to spring directly from her own experience and feelings.

136 *unkind*: unfriendly; *and* unnatural.

139 *blots*: stains.
meads: meadows.

Petruchio
Nay, I will win my wager better yet,
And show more sign of her obedience—
Her new-built virtue and obedience.

Enter Katherina, Bianca, *and* Widow

See where she comes, and brings your froward wives
120 As prisoners to her womanly persuasion.
Katherine, that cap of yours becomes you not:
Off with that bauble—throw it underfoot!

She obeys

Widow
Lord, let me never have a cause to sigh
Till I be brought to such a silly pass!
Bianca
125 Fie, what a foolish duty call you this?
Lucentio
I would your duty were as foolish too.
The wisdom of your duty, fair Bianca,
Hath cost me a hundred crowns since supper-time.
Bianca
The more fool you for laying on my duty.
Petruchio
130 Katherine, I charge thee, tell these headstrong women
What duty they do owe their lords and husbands.
Widow
Come, come, you're mocking. We will have no telling.
Petruchio
Come on, I say, and first begin with her.
Widow
She shall not.
Petruchio
135 I say she shall. And first begin with her.
Katherina
Fie, fie, unknit that threatening unkind brow,
And dart not scornful glances from those eyes
To wound thy lord, thy king, thy governor.
It blots thy beauty as frosts do bite the meads,

'Thy husband is thy lord, thy life, thy keeper' (5, 2, 146). Josie Lawrence as Katherina, Royal Shakespeare Company, 1995.

140 *Confounds thy fame*: destroys your
      reputation.
141 *meet*: appropriate.
142 *mov'd*: bad-tempered.
143 *bereft*: robbed.

147 *Thy head*: See Ephesians, 5:23: 'the
      husband is the head of the wife, even
      as Christ is the head of the Church'.

150 *watch*: be on watch through.

155 *the subject*: See Ephesians, 5:24: 'as
      the Church is subject unto Christ, so
      let the wives be to their own husbands
      in everything'.
158 *honest*: honourable.

161 *so simple*: so simple-minded as.

166 *Unapt to*: unfitted for.
167 *soft conditions*: gentle natures.

169 *unable*: impotent.
170 *big*: arrogant.
171 *haply*: perhaps.
172 *bandy*: exchange, hit back and forth
      (as at tennis).

174 *past compare*: beyond comparison.
175 *That . . . are*: seeming to be most that
      (i.e. strong) which we in fact are least.
176 *vail*: suppress, lower (a metaphor from
      the flags of sailing-ships).
      stomachs: pride, temper.
      no boot: no use, no good.

---

140 Confounds thy fame as whirlwinds shake fair buds,
       And in no sense is meet or amiable.
       A woman mov'd is like a fountain troubled,
       Muddy, ill-seeming, thick, bereft of beauty,
       And while it is so, none so dry or thirsty
145 Will deign to sip, or touch one drop of it.
       Thy husband is thy lord, thy life, thy keeper,
       Thy head, thy sovereign; one that cares for thee
       And for thy maintenance; commits his body
       To painful labour both by sea and land,
150 To watch the night in storms, the day in cold,
       Whilst thou li'st warm at home, secure and safe,
       And craves no other tribute at thy hands
       But love, fair looks, and true obedience—
       Too little payment for so great a debt.
155 Such duty as the subject owes the prince,
       Even such a woman oweth to her husband.
       And when she is froward, peevish, sullen, sour,
       And not obedient to his honest will,
       What is she but a foul contending rebel
160 And graceless traitor to her loving lord?
       I am asham'd that women are so simple
       To offer war where they should kneel for peace,
       Or seek for rule, supremacy, and sway,
       When they are bound to serve, love, and obey.
165 Why are our bodies soft, and weak, and smooth,
       Unapt to toil and trouble in the world,
       But that our soft conditions and our hearts
       Should well agree with our external parts?
       Come, come, you froward and unable worms,
170 My mind hath been as big as one of yours,
       My heart as great, my reason haply more,
       To bandy word for word and frown for frown.
       But now I see our lances are but straws,
       Our strength as weak, our weakness past compare,
175 That seeming to be most which we indeed least are.
       Then vail your stomachs, for it is no boot,
       And place your hands below your husband's foot.
       In token of which duty, if he please,
       My hand is ready, may it do him ease.

Petruchio

180 Why, there's a wench! Come on and kiss me, Kate.

Lucentio

Well, go thy ways, old lad, for thou shall ha't.

Vincentio

'Tis a good hearing when children are toward.

Lucentio

But a harsh hearing when women are froward.

Petruchio

Come, Kate, we'll to bed.

185 We three are married, but you two are sped.

[*To* Lucentio] 'Twas I won the wager, though you hit
   the white,

And being a winner, God give you good night.

                              [*Exeunt* Petruchio *and* Katherina

Hortensio

Now, go thy ways; thou hast tam'd a curst shrew.

Lucentio

'Tis a wonder, by your leave, she will be tam'd so.

                                        [*Exeunt*

180 *kiss me, Kate*: This third kiss confirms the new partnership (compare *2*, 1, 316 and *5*, 1, 121).

181 *go thy ways*: well done.
   ha't: have it—the prize; Petruchio has won the wager.

182 *a good hearing*: good news.
   toward: obedient.

183 *a harsh hearing*: bad news.
   froward: wayward; the couplets which end the play are disappointingly banal.

185 *We three*: i.e. himself, Lucentio, and Hortensio.
   you two: i.e. Lucentio and Hortensio.
   sped: ruined.

186 *the white*: the centre of the target in archery; *also* Bianca, the Italian for 'white'.

187 *being a winner*: whilst I am still winning.

189 *by your leave*: if you don't mind my saying so.

Appendix A

Christopher Sly

After *Act 1*, Scene 1 of *The Taming of the Shrew*, Shakespeare seems to have forgotten about Christopher Sly and the trickster Lord. But a dramatist completed the deception of the tinker in *The Taming of A Shrew*, a play which seems to be an imitation of Shakespeare's. Here the Lord is addressed as 'Sim'—Simon—although it is possible that this was the name of the actor who played the part. These are the major episodes which complete the 'framework'.

1.   *A Shrew*, scene v—after the marriage with Kate has been arranged.

> *Then Sly speaks*

> **Sly**
> Sim, when will the fool come again?
> > **Lord**
> > He'll come again, my lord, anon.
> **Sly**
> Gi's some more drink here. Zounds, where's the tapster?
> Here, Sim, eat some of these things.
> > **Lord**
> > So I do, my lord.
> **Sly**
> Here, Sim: I drink to thee!
> > **Lord**
> > My lord, here comes the players again.
> **Sly**
> O brave! Here's two fine gentlewomen.

2.   *A Shrew*, scene xiv—following the marriage of Kate's two sisters.
> **Sly**
> Sim, must they be married now?
> > **Lord**
> > Ay, my lord.
> **Sly**
> Look, Sim, the fool is come again now.

3.   *A Shrew*, scene xvi—the imposters are condemned to prison, and
        they run away (compare, 5, 1, 91s.d.)

> *Then* Sly *speaks*

> **Sly**
> I say we'll have no sending to prison.
>   **Lord**
> My lord, this is but the play; they're but in jest.
>   **Sly**
> I tell thee Sim, we'll have no sending to prison, that's flat. Why, Sim,
> am I not Don Christo Vary? Therefore I say they shall not go to
> prison.
>   **Lord**
> No more they shall, my lord; they be run away.
>   **Sly**
> Are they run away, Sim? That's well. Then gi's some more to drink,
> and let them play again.

> Sly *drinks, and then falls asleep*

4.   *A Shrew*, scene xvi—between *Act 5*, Scenes 1 and 2 of *The Shrew*.

> Sly *sleeps*

> **Lord**
> Who's within there? Come hither sirs; my lord's
> Asleep again; go, take him easily up,
> And put him in his own apparel again,
> And lay him in the place where we did find him
> Just underneath the alehouse side below.
> But see you wake him not in any case.
>   **Boy**
> It shall be done, my lord. Come, help to bear him hence.

5.   *A Shrew*, scene xix—an Epilogue to the main action.

> *Then enter two bearing* Sly *in his own apparel again, and leaves
> him where they found him; and then goes out.*

Then enter the Tapster

Tapster
Now that the darksome night is overpast,
And dawning day appears in crystal sky,
Now must I haste abroad. But soft, who's this?
What, Sly! O wondrous, hath he lain here all night?
I'll wake him: I think he's starved by this,
But that his belly was so stuffed with ale.
What, how, Sly! Awake, for shame!
Sly
Sim, gi's some more wine—what's all the players gone? Am I not a lord?
Tapster
A lord with a murrain! Come, art thou drunken still?
Sly
Who's this? Tapster! O Lord, sirrah, I have had the bravest dream tonight that ever thou heardest in all thy life.
Tapster
Ay, marry, but you had best get you home, for your wife will curse you for dreaming here tonight.
Sly
Will she? I know now how to tame a shrew: I dreamed upon it all this night till now, and thou hast waked me out of the best dream that ever I had in my life. But I'll to my wife presently, and tame her too, if she anger me.
Tapster
Nay, tarry Sly, for I'll go home with thee,
And hear the rest that thou hast dreamed tonight.

Exeunt omnes

Appendix B

Manning a Hawk

In *Act 4*, Scene 1 Petruchio describes Katherina as a 'haggard'—a wild hawk. Confiding in the audience, he describes the strategies he will employ 'to man my haggard, To make her come and know her keeper's call' (175–6). His methods would be familiar to his Elizabethan audience—and they are still in use today.

Gervase Markham, in *Country Pursuits* (1615), describes the standard technique for training a wild hawk in order to make her 'meek and loving to the man':

> All hawks generally are manned after one manner, that is to say, by watching and keeping them from sleep, by a continual carrying of them upon your fist, and by a most familiar stroking and playing with them, with the wing of a dead fowl or such like, and by often gazing and looking of them in the face, with a loving and gentle countenance, and so making them acquainted with the man.

In *A Kestrel for a Knave*, by Barry Hines (Michael Joseph, 1968), Billy Casper describes the same process to his schoolmates. The scene is a schoolroom in an industrial town in the north of England, sometime in the middle of the twentieth century.

Mr Farthing rested his elbows on his desk and tapped his teeth with his thumb nails, waiting for Billy to collect himself.
   'Now then, Billy, tell us about this hawk. Where did you get it from?'
   'Found it.'
   'Where?'
   'In t'wood.'
   'What had happened to it? Was it injured or something?'
   'It was a young 'un. It must have tumbled from a nest.'
   'And how long have you had it?'
   'Since last year.'
   'All that time? Where do you keep it?'
   'In a shed.'
   'And what do you feed it on?'
   'Beef. Mice. Birds.'

'Isn't it cruel though, keeping it in a shed all the time? Wouldn't it be happier flying free?'

Billy looked at Mr Farthing for the first time since he had told him to sit down.

'I don't keep it in t'shed all t'time. I fly it every day.'

'And doesn't it fly away? I thought hawks were wild birds.'

''Course it don't fly away. I've trained it.'

Billy looked round, as though daring anyone to challenge this authority.

'Trained it? I thought you'd to be an expert to train hawks.'

'Well I did it.'

'Was it difficult?'

''Course it was. You've to be right . . . right patient wi' 'em and take your time.'

'Well tell me how you did it then. I've never met a falconer before, I suppose I must be in select company.'

Billy hutched his chair up and leaned forward over his desk.

'Well what you do is, you train 'em through their stomachs. You can only do owt wi' 'em when they're hungry, so you do all your training at feeding times.

'I started training Kes after I'd had her about a fortnight, when she was hard penned, that means her tail feathers and wing feathers had gone hard at their bases. You have to use a torch at night and keep inspecting 'em. It's easy if you're quiet, you just go up to her as she's roosting, and spread her tail and wings. If t'feathers are blue near t'bottom o' t'shaft, that means there's blood in 'em and they're still soft, so they're not ready yet. When they're white and hard then they're ready, an' you can start training her then.

'Kes wa' as fat as a pig though at first. All young hawks are when you first start to train 'em, and you can't do much wi' 'em 'til you've got their weight down. You've to be ever so careful though, you don't just starve 'em, you weigh 'em before every meal and gradually cut their food down, 'til you go in one time an' she's keen, an' that's when you start getting somewhere. I could tell wi' Kes, she jumped straight on my glove as I held it towards her. So while she wa' feeding I got hold of her jesses an' . . .'

'Her what?'

'Jesses.'

'Jesses. How do you spell that?'

Mr Farthing stood up and stepped back to the board.

'Er, J-E-S-S-E-S.'

As Billy enunciated each letter, Mr Farthing linked them together on the blackboard.

'Jesses. And what are jesses, Billy?'

'They're little leather straps that you fasten round its legs as soon as you get it. She wears these all t'time, and you get hold of 'em when she sits on your glove. You push your swivel through . . .'

'Whoa! Whoa!'

Mr Farthing held up his hands as though Billy was galloping towards him.

'You'd better come out here and give us a demonstration. We're not all experts you know.'

Billy stood up and walked out, taking up position at the side of Mr Farthing's desk. Mr Farthing reared his chair on to its back legs, swivelled it sideways on one leg, then lowered it on to all fours facing Billy.

'Right, off you go.'

'Well, when she stands on your fist, you pull her jesses down between your fingers.'

Billy held his left fist out and drew the jesses down between his first and second fingers.

'Then you get your swivel, like a swivel on a dog lead, press both jesses together, and thread 'em through t'top ring of it. T'jesses have little slits in 'em near t'bottom, like buttonholes in braces, and when you've got t'jesses through t'top ring o' t'swivel, you open these slits with your finger, and push t'bottom ring through, just like fastening a button.'

With the swivel now attached to the jesses, Billy turned to Mr Farthing.

'Do you see?'

'Yes, I see. Carry on.'

'Well when you've done that, you thread your leash, that's a leather thong, through t'bottom ring o' t'swivel . . .'

Billy carefully threaded the leash, grabbed the loose end as it penetrated the ring, and pulled it through.

'. . . until it binds on t'knot at t'other end. Have you got that?'

'Yes, I think so. Just let me get it right. The jesses round the hawk's legs are attached to a swivel, which is then attached to a lead . . .'

'A leash!'

'Leash, sorry. Then what?'

'You wrap your leash round your fingers and tie it on to your little finger.'

'So that the hawk is now attached to your hand?'

'That's right. Well, when you've reached this stage and it's stepping on to your glove regular, and feeding all right and not bating too much . . .'

'Bating? What's that?'

'Trying to fly off; in a panic like.'

'How do you spell it?'

'B-A-T-I-N-G.'

'Carry on.'

'Well, when you've reached this stage inside, you can try feeding her outside and getting her used to other things. You call this manning. That means taming, and you've got to have her well manned before you can start training her right.'

While Billy was talking, Mr Farthing reached out and slowly printed on the board B A T I N G; watching Billy all the time as though he was a hawk, and that any sudden movement, or rasp of chalk would make him bate from the side of the desk.

'You take her out at night first and don't go near anybody. I used to walk her round t'fields at t'back of our house at first, then as she got less nervous I started to bring her out in t'day and then take her near other folks, and dogs and cats and cars and things. You've to be ever so careful when you're outside though, 'cos hawks are right nervous and they've got fantastic eyesight, and things are ten times worse for them than they are for us. So you've to be right patient, an' all t'time you're walking her you've to talk to her, all soft like, like you do to a baby.'

He paused for breath. Mr Farthing nodded him on before he had time to become self-conscious.

'Well, when you've manned her, you can start training her right then. You can tell when she's ready, 'cos she looks forward to you comin' an' there's no trouble gettin' her on to your glove. Not like at first when she's bating all t'time.

'You start inside first, makin' her jump on to your glove for her meat. Only a little jump at first, then a bit further and so on; and every time she comes you've to give her a scrap o' meat. A reward like. When she'll come about a leash length straight away, you can try her outside, off a fence post or summat like that. You put her down, hold on to t'end of your leash wi' your right hand, and hold your glove out for her to fly to. This way you can get a double leash length. After she's done this, you can take her leash off an' attach a creance in its place.'

'Creance?'

Mr Farthing leaned over to the blackboard.

'C-R-E-A-N-C-E—it's a long line, I used a long nylon fishing line wi' a clasp off a dog lead, tied to one end. Well, you clip this to your swivel, pull your leash out, and put your hawk down on a fence post. Then you walk away into t'field unwindin' your creance, an' t'hawk sits there waitin' for you to stop an' hold your glove up. It's so it can't fly away, you see.'

'Yes I see. It all sounds very skilful and complicated, Billy.'

'It don't sound half as bad as it is though. I've just told you in a couple o' minutes how to carry on, but it takes weeks to go through all them stages. They're as stubborn as mules, hawks, they're right tempr . . . tempr . . .'

'Temperamental.'

'Temperamental. Sometimes she'd be all right, then next time I'd go in, she'd go mad, screamin' an' batin' as though she'd never seen me before. You'd think you'd learnt her summat, an' put her away feelin' champion, then t'next time you went you were back where you started. You just couldn't reckon it up at all.'

He looked down at Mr Farthing, eyes animated, cheeks flushed under a wash of smeared tears and dirt.

'You make it sound very exciting though.'

'It is, Sir. But most exciting thing wa' when I flew her free first time. You ought to have been there then. I wa' frightened to death.'

Mr Farthing turned to the class, rotating his trunk without moving his chair.

'Do you want to hear about it?'

Chorus: 'Yes, Sir.'

Mr Farthing smiled and turned back to Billy.

'Carry on, Casper.'

'Well I'd been flyin' it on t'creance for about a week, an' it wa' comin' back to me owt up to thirty, forty yards, an' it says in t'books that when it's comin' this far, straight away, it's ready to fly loose. I daren't though. I kep' sayin' to missen, I'll just use t'creance today to make sure, then I'll fly it free tomorrow. But when tomorrow came I did t'smack same thing. I did this for about four days an' I got right mad wi' missen 'cos I knew I'd have to do it sometime. So on t'last day I didn't feed her up, just to make sure that she'd be sharp set next morning. I hardly went to sleep that night, I wa' thinking about it that much.

'It wa' on Friday night, an' when I got up next morning I thought right, if she flies off, she flies off, an' it can't be helped. So I went down to t'shed. She wa' dead keen an' all, walking about on her shelf behind t'bars, an' screamin' out when she saw me comin'. So I took her out in t'field and tried her on t'creance first time, an' she came like a rocket. So I thought, right, this time.

'I unclipped t'creance, took t'swivel off an' let her hop on to t'fence post. There was nowt stoppin' her now, she wa' just standin' there wi' her jesses on. She could have took off an' there wa' nowt I could have done about it. I wa' terrified. I thought she's forced to go, she's forced to, she'll just fly an' that'll be it. But she didn't. She just sat there looking round while I backed off into t'field. I went right into t'middle, then held my glove up an' shouted her.'

Billy held his left fist up and stared out of the window.

'Come on, Kes! Come on then! Nowt happened at first, then, just when I wa' going to walk back to her, she came. You ought to have seen her. Straight as a die, about a yard off t'floor. An' t' speed . . . She came like lightnin', head dead still, an' her wings never made a sound, then wham! Straight up on to t'glove, claws out grabbin' for t'meat,' simultaneously demonstrating the last yard of her flight with his right hand, gliding it towards, then slapping it down on his raised fist.

'I wa' that pleased I didn't know what to do wi' missen, so I thought just to prove it, I'll try her again, an' she came t'second time just as good. Well that was it. I'd done it. I'd trained her.'

(This extract is published by kind permission of Michael Joseph Ltd, © 1968 by Barry Hines.)

Classwork and Examinations

The works of Shakespeare are studied all over the world, and this classroom edition is being used in many different countries. Teaching methods vary from school to school—even *within* the United Kingdom—and there are many different ways of examining a student's work. Some teachers and examiners expect detailed knowledge of Shakespeare's text; others ask for imaginative involvement with his characters and their situations; and there are some teachers who want their students, by means of 'workshop' activities, to share in the theatrical experience of directing and performing a play. Most people use a variety of methods. This section of the book offers a few suggestions for approaches to *The Taming of the Shrew* which could be used in schools and colleges to help with students' understanding and *enjoyment* of the play.

A   Discussion of Themes and Topics
B   Character Study
C   Activities
D   Context Questions
E   Critical Appreciation
F   Essays
G   Projects

A   Discussion of Themes and Topics

It is most sensible to discuss each scene as it is read, sharing impressions (and perhaps correcting misapprehensions): no two people experience any character in quite the same way, and we all have different expectations. It can be useful to compare aspects of this play with other fictions—plays, novels, films—or with modern life. A large class should divide into small groups, each with a leader, who can discuss different aspects of a single topic and then report back to the main assembly.

Suggestions

A1   Christopher Sly has 'never heard a play' (*Induction*, Scene 1, line 92). How would you describe plays—both comedies and tragedies—to someone who knows nothing about drama? Are plays anything more than entertainment? Is there any difference between seeing a play at the theatre and watching a film at the cinema or on television?

A2   Baptista arranges the marriages of both his daughters. Can you think of any other 'arranged marriages' in fiction? Do such marriages happen in the twenty-first century? Do you think parents should be able to influence their children in this way?

A3   Tranio asks 'is it possible That love should of a sudden take such hold?' (1, 1, 143–4). Do you believe in love at first sight?

A4   Baptista arranges for his daughters to have tuition in literature and music. Do you think it is necessary to have some knowledge of arts subjects?

A5   Some of Shakespeare's characters (for instance Gremio, the 'pantaloon') are well-known stock figures from the conventions of the *commedia dell'arte*. What character stereotypes do we recognize today—in plays, films, and television?

A6   If you were to stage this play, would you put the characters in modern dress? What would be the advantages and the drawbacks?

B   Character Study   Shakespeare's characters can be studied in many different ways, either from the *outside*, where the detached, critical student (or group of students) can see the function of every character within the whole scheme and pattern of the play; or from the *inside*, where the sympathetic student (like an actor) can identify with a single character and can look at the action and the other characters from his/her point of view.

Suggestions   a) from 'outside' the character

B1   Write detailed character studies of
   a) Bianca
   b) Katherina
   c) Petruchio.

B2   At the beginning of the play, Petruchio is a fortune-hunter who has 'come to wive it wealthily in Padua' (1, 2, 72). Show how the character develops from this point.

B3   'They deserve each other'. Could this be said of *either* Katherina and Petruchio, *or* Bianca and Lucentio?

B4   Ben Jonson (a contemporary dramatist) said that Shakespeare 'was not of an age, but for all time'. What 'timeless' qualities do you particularly notice in the characters of *The Taming of the Shrew*?

B5 What functions are served by the comic servants (Tranio, Grumio, and Biondello)?

b) from 'inside' the character

B6 As Baptista, write letters to an old friend in another town describing:
   a) your two daughters and your hopes (and fears) about their futures
   b) the wedding of Katherina
   c) the amazing transformation of Katherina after her marriage.

B7 In the character of Bianca, writing to a girl-friend, describe
   a) your sister
   b) your new tutors
   c) Katherina's wedding.

B8 In Katherina's personal diary, confide your thoughts about
   a) your father
   b) your sister and her suitors
   c) Petruchio, both before and after your wedding.

B9 As one of Petruchio's other servants (i.e. *not* Grumio), describe your master's treatment of his new bride.

B10 Write a letter from the Widow (Hortensio's bride) to one of her old friends, describing the events and personalities at the wedding feast.

C Activities These can involve two or more students, preferably working *away from* the desk or study-table and using gesture and position ('body-language') as well as speech. They can help students to develop a sense of drama and the dramatic aspects of Shakespeare's play—which was written to be *performed*, not studied in a classroom.

Suggestions **C1** Speak the lines—act the scenes! To familiarize yourselves with Shakespeare's verse, try different reading techniques—reading by punctuation marks (where each person hands over to the next at every punctuation mark); reading by sentences; and reading by speeches. Begin acting with small units—about ten lines—where two or three characters are speaking to each other; rehearse these in groups of students, and perform them before the whole class. Read the lines from a script—then act them out in your own words.

C2 Devise some new scenes with Christopher Sly to complete the 'framework' of the play (see Appendix A, p. 114).

C3   Baptista is an important man in Padua, and the wedding of his elder daughter would be widely reported. Give it full 'media coverage' (newspaper, radio, and television), interviewing all who were present—including those who saw nothing but want to appear on television. Research a background for 'The Mysterious Stranger from Verona'.

C4   When it comes, will it come without warning
          Just as I'm picking my nose?
    Will it knock on my door in the morning,
          Or tread in the bus on my toes?
    Will it come like a change in the weather?
          Will its greeting be courteous or rough?
    Will it alter my life altogether?
          O tell me the truth about love.

                                        (W. H. Auden, Song XII)

Organize a classroom debate to answer Auden's question. How would the different male characters—Lucentio, Gremio, Hortensio, and Petruchio—answer? Would Katherina or Bianca be able to tell 'the truth about love'? Is Baptista interested in love? What is the Widow's point of view?

C5   Let one member of the group read aloud Katherina's exhortation to wives ('Fie, fie, unknit that threatening, unkind brow', 5, 2, 136–79) whilst the rest *listen*; then let the others—either representing characters in the play or in their own persons—describe their reactions—how they thought and felt at the time the speech was being read, and what they think afterwards.

D Context Questions   Questions like these, which are sometimes used in written examinations, can also be helpful as a class revision quiz, testing knowledge of the play and some understanding of its words.

D1   Am I a lord, and have I such a lady?
    Or do I dream? Or have I dream'd till now?
    I do not sleep: I see, I hear, I speak,
    I smell sweet savours and I feel soft things.
    Upon my life, I am a lord indeed,

    (i)   Who is speaking?
    (ii) Who is the 'lady' he refers to?
    (iii) Where is he speaking from, and how did he get there?

D2   Why, sir, you know this is your wedding-day.
First were we sad, fearing you would not come,
Now sadder that you come so unprovided.
Fie, doff this habit, shame to your estate,
An eye-sore to our solemn festival!

    (i)   Who is the speaker, and to whom is he speaking?
    (ii)   How is this person 'unprovided'?
    (iii)   What happens next?

D3   Mistake no more—I am not Litio,
Nor a musician as I seem to be,
But one that scorn to live in this disguise
For such a one as leaves a gentleman
And makes a god of such a cullion.

    (i)   What is the speaker's real name?
    (ii)   Who is referred to as 'such a one', and who is described as a 'cullion'?
    (iii)   Whom does the speaker marry?

D4   But after many ceremonies done
He calls for wine. 'A health!' quoth he, as if
He had been aboard, carousing to his mates
After a storm; quaff'd off the muscadel,
And threw the sops all in the sexton's face

    (i)   Who is the speaker, and to whom is he speaking?
    (ii)   What 'ceremonies' have been performed?
    (iii)   Who is the person referred to as 'He'?

D5   I am my father's heir and only son.
If I may have your daughter to my wife,
I'll leave her houses three or four as good
Within rich Pisa walls as any one
Old Signor——has in——.

    (i)   What are the real and assumed names of the speaker?
    (ii)   To whom is he speaking, and which 'daughter' does he refer to?
    (iii)   Who is the 'Old Signor', and in which town are his 'houses'?

E Critical Appreciation   Some examination boards allow candidates to take their copies of the play into the examination room, asking them to re-read specified sections of the play and answer questions on them.

E1   *Act* 2, Scene 1, lines 169–216 ('Say that she rail' . . . 'I swear I'll cuff you if you strike again')
Comment on the humour and the dramatic effectiveness of this passage. How does Petruchio develop a relationship with the audience?

E2   *Induction*, Scene 2, lines 66–125 ('Am I a lord' . . . 'despite of the flesh and the blood')
How does this Induction prepare the audience for the main action of *The Taming of the Shrew*? What does it show you of Elizabethan life and acting convention? Comment on the dramatic and comic potential of the episode.

E3   *Act* 2, Scene 1, lines 324–390 ('But now, Baptista' . . . 'And so I take my leave')
What are your reactions to this 'auctioning' of Bianca?

F   Essays   These will usually give you a specific topic to discuss, or perhaps a question that must be answered, in writing, *with a reasoned argument*. They *never* want you to tell the story of the play—so don't! Your examiner—or teacher—has read the play and does not need to be reminded of it. Relevant quotations will always help you to make your points more strongly.

Suggested Topics   **F1**   ''Tis a wonder, by your leave, she will be tam'd so' (5, 2, 189). Do you share Lucentio's scepticism about the success of Petruchio's 'taming' of Katherina?

F2   Do you think—on the evidence of this play—that Shakespeare was anti-feminist?

F3   Examine Shakespeare's use of prose and verse in *The Taming of the Shrew*.

F4   Do you agree with Anne Barton that 'at the end of the play, Katherina is a woman who has discovered, and come to terms with, her own genuine nature'?

F5   Discuss the theme of appearance and reality in *The Taming of the Shrew*.

G Projects In some schools, students are asked to do more 'free-ranging' work, which takes them outside the text—but which should always be relevant to the play. Such Projects may demand skills other than reading and writing; design and artwork, for instance, may be involved. Sometimes a 'portfolio' of work is assembled over a considerable period of time; and this can be presented to the examiner as part of the student's work for assessment.

The availability of resources will, obviously, do much to determine the nature of the Projects; but this is something that only the local teachers will understand. However, there is always help to be found in libraries, museums, and art galleries.

G1 Arranged marriages.

G2 Past productions of *The Taming of the Shrew*.

G3 Costumes for *The Taming of the Shrew*.

G4 'The Battle of the Sexes'.

G5 The *Commedia dell'arte*.

G6 Actors on Tour.

Background

England c. 1592

When Shakespeare was writing *The Taming of the Shrew*, most people believed that the sun went round the earth. They were taught that this was a divinely ordered scheme of things, and that—in England—God had instituted a Church and ordained a Monarchy for the right government of the land and the populace.

'The past is a foreign country; they do things differently there.'

L. P. Hartley

Government For most of Shakespeare's life, the reigning monarch of England was Queen Elizabeth I. With her counsellors and ministers, she governed the country (population about five million) from London, although fewer than half a million people inhabited the capital city. In the rest of the country, law and order were maintained by the land-owners and enforced by their deputies. The average man had no vote, and his wife had no rights at all.

Religion At this time, England was a Christian country. All children were baptized, soon after they were born, into the Church of England; they were taught the essentials of the Christian faith, and instructed in their duty to God and to humankind. Marriages were performed, and funerals conducted, only by the licensed clergy and in accordance with the Church's rites and ceremonies. Attendance at divine service was compulsory; absences (without good—medical—reason) could be punished by fines. By such means, the authorities were able to keep some check on the populace—recording births, marriages, and deaths; being alert to any religious nonconformity, which could be politically dangerous; and ensuring a minimum of orthodox instruction through the official 'Homilies' which were regularly preached from the pulpits of all parish churches throughout the realm. Following Henry VIII's break away from the Church of Rome, all people in England were able to hear the church services *in their own language*. The Book of Common Prayer was used in every church, and an English translation of the Bible was read aloud in public. The Christian religion had never been so well taught before!

Education   School education reinforced the Church's teaching. From the age of four, boys might attend the 'petty school' (French '*petite école*') to learn the rudiments of reading and writing along with a few prayers; some schools also included work with numbers. At the age of seven, the boy was ready for the grammar school (if his father was willing and able to pay the fees).

Here, a thorough grounding in Latin grammar was followed by translation work and the study of Roman authors, paying attention as much to style as to matter. The arts of fine writing were thus inculcated from early youth. A very few students proceeded to university; these were either clever scholarship boys, or else the sons of noblemen. Girls stayed at home, and acquired domestic and social skills—cooking, sewing, perhaps even music. The lucky ones might learn to read and write.

Language   At the start of the sixteenth century the English had a very poor opinion of their own language: there was little serious writing in English, and hardly any literature. Latin was the language of international scholarship, and Englishmen admired the eloquence of the Romans. They made many translations, and in this way they extended the resources of their own language, increasing its vocabulary and stretching its grammatical structures. French, Italian, and Spanish works were also translated and—for the first time—there were English versions of the Bible. By the end of the century, English was a language to be proud of: it was rich in synonyms, capable of infinite variety and subtlety, and ready for all kinds of word-play—especially the *puns*, for which Elizabethan English is renowned.

Drama   The great art-form of the Elizabethan age was its drama. The Elizabethans inherited a tradition of play-acting from the Middle Ages, and they reinforced this by reading and translating the Roman playwrights. At the beginning of the sixteenth century, plays were performed by groups of actors, all-male companies (boys acted the female roles) who travelled from town to town, setting up their stages in open places (such as inn-yards) or, with the permission of the owner, in the hall of some noble house. The touring companies continued, in the provinces, into the seventeenth century; but in London, in 1576, a new building was erected for the performance of plays. This was the Theatre, the first purpose-built playhouse in England. Other playhouses followed, (including Shakespeare's own theatre, the Globe) and the English drama reached new heights of eloquence.

There were those who disapproved, of course. The theatres, which brought large crowds together, could encourage the spread of disease—and dangerous ideas. During the summer, when the plague was at its worst, the playhouses were closed. A constant censorship was imposed, more or less severe at different times. The Puritan faction tried to close down the theatres, but—partly because there was royal favour for the drama, and partly because the buildings were outside the city limits—they did not succeed until 1642.

Theatre   From contemporary comments and sketches—most particularly a drawing by a Dutch visitor, Johannes de Witt—it is possible to form some idea of the typical Elizabethan playhouse for which most of Shakespeare's plays were written. Hexagonal in shape, it had three roofed galleries encircling an open courtyard. The plain, high stage projected into the yard, where it was surrounded by the audience of standing 'groundlings'. At the back were two doors for the actors' entrances and exits, and between these doors was a curtained 'discovery space' (sometimes called an 'inner stage'). Above this was a balcony, used as a musicians' gallery or for the performance of scenes 'above', and projecting over part of the stage was a roof, supported on two pillars, which was painted with the sun, moon, and stars for the 'heavens'. Underneath was space (concealed by curtaining) which could be used by characters ascending and descending through a trap-door in the stage. Costumes and properties were kept backstage in the 'tiring house'. The actors dressed lavishly, often wearing the secondhand clothes bestowed by rich patrons. Stage properties were important for defining a location, but the dramatist's own words were needed to explain the time of day, since all performances took place in the early afternoon.

A replica of Shakespeare's own theatre, the Globe, has been built in London, and stands in Southwark, almost exactly on the Bankside site of the original.

Shakespeare's Globe, Southwark, London, England. Photograph by Richard Kalina.

Selected Further Reading

Berry, Ralph, *Shakespeare's Comedies*, (Princeton University Press, 1972).

Dusinberre, Juliet, *Shakespeare and the Nature of Women*, (London, 1975).

Leggatt, Alexander, *Shakespeare's Comedy of Love*, (London, 1974).

Nevo, Ruth, *Comic Transformations in Shakespeare*, (Methuen, 1980).

Salinger, Leo, *Shakespeare and the Traditions of Comedy*, (Cambridge, 1974).

Stone, Lawrence, *The Family, Sex and Marriage in England 1500–1800*, (1977).

Sources: Muir, Kenneth, *The Sources of Shakespeare's Plays* (London, 1977).

Additional Background Reading: Bate, Jonathan, *The Genius of Shakespeare* (Picador [Macmillan], 1997).

Blake, N. F., *Shakespeare's Language: an Introduction* (London, 1983).

Gibson, Rex, *Shakespeare's Language* (Cambridge, 1997).

Honan, Park, *Shakespeare: A Life* (Oxford, 1998).

Langley, Andrew, *Shakespeare's Theatre* (Oxford, 1999).

Muir, K., and Schoenbaum, S., *A New Companion to Shakespeare Studies* (Cambridge, 1971).

Thomson, Peter, *Shakespeare's Theatre* (London, 1983).

William Shakespeare, 1564–1616

Elizabeth I was Queen of England when Shakespeare was born in 1564. He was the son of a tradesman who made and sold gloves in the small town of Stratford-upon-Avon, and he was educated at the grammar school in that town. Shakespeare did not go to university when he left school, but worked, perhaps, in his father's business. When he was eighteen he married Anne Hathaway, who became the mother of his daughter, Susanna, in 1583, and of twins in 1585.

There is nothing exciting, or even unusual, in this story; and from 1585 until 1592 there are no documents that can tell us anything at all about Shakespeare. But we have learned that in 1592 he was known in London, and that he had become both an actor and a playwright.

We do not know when Shakespeare wrote his first play, and indeed we are not sure of the order in which he wrote his works. If you look on page 137 at the list of his writings and their approximate dates, you will see how he started by writing plays on subjects taken from the history of England. No doubt this was partly because he was always an intensely patriotic man—but he was also a very shrewd businessman. He could see that the theatre audiences enjoyed being shown their own history, and it was certain that he would make a profit from this kind of drama.

The plays in the next group are mainly comedies, with romantic love-stories of young people who fall in love with one another, and at the end of the play marry and live happily ever after.

At the end of the sixteenth century the happiness disappears, and Shakespeare's plays become melancholy, bitter, and tragic. This change may have been caused by some sadness in the writer's life (one of his twins died in 1596). Shakespeare, however, was not the only writer whose works at this time were very serious. The whole of England was facing a crisis. Queen Elizabeth I was growing old. She was greatly loved, and the people were sad to think she must soon die; they were also afraid, for the queen had never married, and so there was no child to succeed her.

When James I came to the throne in 1603, Shakespeare continued to write serious drama—the great tragedies and the plays based on Roman history (such as *Julius Caesar*) for which he is most famous. Finally, before he retired from the theatre, he wrote another set of comedies. These all have the same theme: they tell of happiness which is lost, and then found again.

Shakespeare returned from London to Stratford, his home town. He was rich and successful, and he owned one of the biggest houses in the town. He died in 1616. Although several of his plays were published separately, most of them were not printed until 1623, in a collection known as 'the First Folio'.

Shakespeare also wrote two long poems, and a collection of sonnets. The sonnets describe two love-affairs, but we do not know who the lovers were. Although there are many public documents concerned with his career as a writer and a businessman, Shakespeare has hidden his personal life from us. A nineteenth-century poet, Matthew Arnold, addressed Shakespeare in a poem, and wrote 'We ask and ask—Thou smilest, and art still'.

There is not even a trustworthy portrait of the world's greatest dramatist.

Approximate order of composition of Shakespeare's works

Period	Comedies	History plays	Tragedies	Poems
I	Comedy of Errors Taming of the Shrew	Henry VI, part 1 Henry VI, part 2	Titus Andronicus	
1594	Two Gentlemen of Verona Love's Labour's Lost	Henry VI, part 3 Richard III King John		Venus and Adonis Rape of Lucrece
II	Midsummer Night's Dream Merchant of Venice	Richard II Henry IV, part 1	Romeo and Juliet	
1599	Merry Wives of Windsor Much Ado About Nothing As You Like It	Henry IV, part 2 Henry V		Sonnets
III	Twelfth Night Troilus and Cressida		Julius Caesar Hamlet	
1608	Measure for Measure All's Well That Ends Well		Othello Timon of Athens King Lear Macbeth Antony and Cleopatra Coriolanus	
IV	Pericles Cymbeline			
1613	The Winter's Tale The Tempest	Henry VIII		